Julie Andrews

For many people Julie Andrews is still to be taken with a spoonful of sugar – remembered for her Mary Poppins, her Eliza in *My Fair Lady* or for her universally acclaimed performance as Maria in *The Sound of Music*.

But after several years of professional exile Julie Andrews is back – adopting a sensationally different image from that of the English rose she so perfectly embodied.

In this up-dated biography Robert Windeler, former Hollywood correspondent and bestselling author of *Sweetheart: The Story of Mary Pickford*, takes a retrospective look at her career and re-examines her contribution to the entertainment world. He attempts to explain Julie Andrews' retreat from the limelight and the dramatic change of direction she now seems to be taking. His insights into her relationships with Blake Edwards and the influence he has had on her development – professional and personal – make fascinating reading.

D1472879

Also by Robert Windeler
Sweetheart: The Story of Mary Pickford
Shirley Temple
The Party Book
(with Milton Williams)

Robert Windeler

Julie Andrews

A Biography

A COMET BOOK
Published by the Paperback Division of
W.H. ALLEN & CO. LTD

A Comet Book
Published in 1984
by the Paperback Division of
W.H. Allen & Co. Ltd
A Howard and Wyndham Company
44 Hill Street, London W1X 8LB

This revised and up-dated edition is based on
Julie Andrews: A Biography © Robert Windeler, 1973

Copyright © Robert Windeler, 1982

Printed and bound in Great Britain by
Mackays of Chatham Ltd, Kent.

ISBN 0 86379 006 2

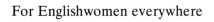

For Englishwomen everywhere

ACKNOWLEDGEMENTS

MANY of Julie Andrews' friends and colleagues were helpful in the research for both editions of this biography. I would particularly like to thank André Previn, Blake Edwards, James Garner, Carol Burnett, Robert Wise, Alan Jay Lerner and John Calley. Hollywood studio publicists who were gracious in their assistance, as always, include Susan Pile at Paramount, Mort Lichter at Warner Brothers, Phyllis Gardner at MGM, Arlene Ludwig at Disney, Fredell Pogodin at Universal and Lloyd Leipzig at Orion. A special thanks to Julie and Blake's publicist, Julian Myers at Hanson and Schwamm.

The work of other journalists has been helpful in the updating of this biography, particularly that of Elaine Liner, George Haddad-Garcia, John Walker, Joan Saunders Wixen and Jane Ardmore.

Julie's fans are among the most loyal of any performer's, and I'm particularly grateful to Kathy Mervine, Sharon Murphy, Kelly Lawrence, Terry Nelson, Tom Wilson and Larry Schmitt for sticking with her (and with me) through the lean years, and for their help with this completely revised work.

CONTENTS

INTRODUCTION

WHEN she was thirteen she sang for the Queen of England, at nineteen she was the toast of Broadway, and before she was thirty, Julie Andrews was the best-loved, highest-paid entertainer in the world. But she was a star before she became a person. 'There was a time when I really did not know who I was myself,' she said. 'So I simply hid behind the roles that I played. Performing gave me a sense of identity.'

Fortunately at the time, perhaps unfortunately in retrospect, most of her successful early roles (particularly in the films *Mary Poppins* and *The Sound of Music*) had a sameness and sweetness that may have made her millions of dollars but also stamped her with an image summed up in a word she would come to hate: wholesome. 'She's got a hell of a cross to bear,' said Blake Edwards, her second husband – they have been married now for twelve years – and her director in five of her last six films. 'I'd hate to be Mary Poppins.'

At the peak of her fame she was unhappy enough to submit to daily psychoanalysis in an attempt to overcome the insecurities brought on by a grim Second World War childhood, and 'to purge oneself of guilt for suddenly having been given so much'. After five years of analysis, she felt she had done that. She married Edwards and said, 'For the first time in my life I was truly happy.' But just as she achieved a semblance of peace with herself, Julie's popularity with the public ended with an inexplicable bang that led to professional exile from Hollywood for herself and her husband for several years. She re-entered the world of show business from time to time (mostly in films made by her husband), but from the age of thirty-six to forty-six she concentrated on her children and home life 'until the family agreed it was time for Mummy to go back to work'.

While her current movies, *S.O.B.* and *Victor/Victoria* are as different from her early work as it is possible to be without being unambiguously pornographic, in the popular imagination Julie Andrews still represents the essence of innocence and the nanny next door. She was not conventionally pretty or sexy, and her major career asset for forty years seemed to be her crystalline five-octave singing voice. Her former secretary, who had worked for Joan Fontaine and Zsa Zsa Gabor and intercepted many marriage proposals for them, said Julie received not a single one in the morning mail.

Her fall from grace might seem equally unfathomable, since she remained a major part of the public consciousness in entertainment in the 1980s, as she had in the 1970s and 1960s (and the 1950s on Broadway, and even the 1940s in London) – even though she had long ceased to sell many tickets.

'It's a cycle,' she said, 'nobody and nothing in this life is forever, and generations replace each other. I don't know if many stars view movies as a way of gaining immortality, because that's a rather shallow view. Only a few people are remembered from each century and most of them do things far more important than act in films.'

Despite the setbacks of her life in and out of the public eye, Julie said, 'I'm not bitter about a thing, and if I were, what would it gain me? I'm glad to have broken away from the demands of that early stardom. But does any of us ever find out who we really are? Aren't we all groping, searching all our lives?'

This is the story of her search, but it is also the story of the career of Julie Andrews. For, while she may ultimately have found more contentment in domesticity, she realized that, so far as the public were concerned, 'In the long run it is a person's body of work that matters. If it is honest, with an integrity about it, and people sense a love of work in it, those are the things that last and that one is remembered for, possibly.'

1

BANDY LEGS, BUCK TEETH AND A FREAK VOICE

JULIA ELIZABETH WELLS was born in Walton-on-Thames, Surrey, eighteen miles south of London, on 1 October 1935. She was named after her two grandmothers, Julia Morris and Elizabeth Wells, but it was not long before she became 'Julie'.

Her father, Edward C. 'Ted' Wells, was a teacher of woodwork and metalcraft in a state school. Her mother, Barbara Morris Wells, who was also born in Walton, was a part-time pianist for an evening dance-school run by her sister, Joan, who lived with the Wellses in modest but not poverty-stricken circumstances. The dance classes (one shilling for a half hour) were held in a building that served as a private preparatory school by day. When Barbara Wells played the piano for the dance classes, she took the infant Julie along with her in a pram. Her father recalled that Julie saw dancing and heard music long before anyone thought about her walking or talking.

'My mum, when she was younger, had been a very promising concert pianist,' said Julie, 'but her parents died when they were young, and she had to quit studying to raise her younger sister.'

It was that same sister, Joan, who gave Julie her first parts on stage. When she was two she appeared in the dancing school's pageant in the non-speaking role of a fairy. The next year Julie had her first singing and speaking part: as Nod in the school's production of *Winken, Blinken and Nod*. Ted Wells built the nursery set, and Barbara Wells played the piano, as usual.

Just before Great Britain entered the Second World War, in the summer of 1939, when Julie was not quite four, Barbara Wells took a job as the pianist for a variety show, the Dazzle Company, at a seaside music hall at Bognor Regis. On the bill, as a last-minute substitute act, was 'The Canadian Troubador, Songs and a Guitar'. The songs were sung, in a rich tenor voice, and the guitar was played, by a Canadian, Ted Andrews, who had emigrated to England as a vaudeville entertainer.

None of the principals ever talked about what happened next, and Julie said, 'I don't remember anything because I was kept in the dark about it all.' But war did break out, and Bognor Regis emptied; the younger men of the cast and crew of the Dazzle Company were drafted. Barbara Wells and Ted Andrews together joined an ENSA (Entertainments National Services Association) company to entertain troops.

Ted Wells first helped with the evacuation of schoolchildren in Surrey, then worked in a war factory in Hinchley Wood. There he met Winifred, the woman who was to become his second wife; she was a hairdresser, training to operate a lathe. The Wellses were divorced; Barbara married Ted Andrews, and Ted Wells married his 'Win'.

Wells got custody of Julie and her younger brother, John, but voluntarily returned Julie to her mother when he decided that 'with war work taking up so much of my time, I could not do my duty to both of them as a father'. His other considerations, he recalled, were that 'a growing girl needs a mother's

Singing practice with 'Pop', stepfather Ted Andrews
1947 PICTORIAL PARADE

influence', and that Barbara and Andrews 'being in the theatre themselves were better equipped than I to pay for her training'. Wells said he had determined from the children's earliest theatricals that his daughter belonged on stage.

The separation, divorce and subsequent custody arrangements were accomplished amicably – on the surface at least. 'There were no fights, no loud scenes, thank God,' Julie recalled. 'The next thing I knew, a personality as colourful and noisy as show business itself – another Ted – came into my life. He thundered across my childhood.'

So did the Second World War, in the most literal sense. 'I was lucky because we weren't hit, but it was scary at times,' she remembered. 'Sometimes I think I've almost forgotten those childhood memories, and then I go to an utterly beautiful land like Hawaii, and the banging comes back to me all at once.' On the set of *Darling Lili* an actor fired a gun containing blanks, and Julie turned a terrified white. She continued to hate violent noise coming suddenly, a fear that in her 1960s psychoanalysis sessions was traced to a specific blitz during the War.

Julie was 'five or six' when she went to live with her mother and new stepfather, whom she disliked on first meeting. 'My Mum wanted me to call him "Uncle Ted", which I was opposed to instantly,' she said. 'To avoid muddling I did end up calling him "Pop" and my real father "Dad" or "Daddy".'

The new Andrews family (Julie's name was legally changed) at first were 'very poor, and we lived in a bad slum area of London. That was a very black period in my life. I hated my new house and the huge man who seemed to fill it.'

But Ted and Barbara Andrews as a second act in vaudeville began to achieve greater success, and the housing improved. 'We were never top of the bill,' Mrs Andrews recalled. 'After all, we were musical and not comedy, and the comedians got the best billing. But we were the second feature, a good supporting act with a drawing-room set and ballads – nice family-type entertainment.'

By the time Julie was eight, the family had moved to Beckenham, Kent, whose inhabitants tended to ignore most official air-raid warnings and go into shelters only when they actually saw German aeroplanes and 'doodlebugs' (flying-bombs) virtually overhead. Julie was equipped with opera glasses and whistle to watch for doodlebugs and warn the neighbours. Ted Andrews led *a cappella* community singing in the shelters during air raids. One night Julie suddenly joined in the singing, soaring an octave, or sometimes two, above the general pitch.

'In all fairness, I truthfully do not know whether I started in show business because of my parents, or circumstances, or what,' Julie said. 'But I was under everyone's feet. My stepfather, not knowing what to do with me (and I think in an attempt to get closer to me) sent me off to a singing teacher.'

A specialist confirmed that the 'bandy-legged, buck-toothed child' had 'an enormous, belting, freak voice with a range of five octaves and some fierce high notes'.

'I sounded like an immature Yma Sumac,' Julie said.

Ted Andrews was delighted with his stepdaughter's newly discovered talent, and he literally forced her to develop it. He sent her to a new voice teacher, Madame Lilian Stiles-Allen, a renowned concert singer and a 'wonderful woman', who stayed with Julie as friend and coach until long after she was a superstar. 'It's thanks to her that I didn't do more damage to my voice with all that singing, when I was young, and later in *My Fair Lady*,' Julie said. 'I used to go watch her give lessons to all her other pupils, then I would take lessons twice a day. She had an enormous influence on me. She was my third mother.'

Ted Andrews pushed hard. To avoid overstraining her young voice, Julie was 'made to practise singing only a half an hour a day, but it seemed much longer than that. And none of the other girls I knew had to practise singing at all. I loathed singing and resented my stepfather. He acutely embarrassed and upset me by asking me to perform. But he was a very good disciplinarian, and later I was grateful that he had made me take singing lessons. It gave me an identity which later became very necessary. Without it I would have been ten times more mixed up than I was.'

Sometimes Julie attended the Cone-Ripman School in London, which taught acting and ballet in the morning, and more conventional subjects in the afternoon. Her Aunt Joan Morris taught there between sessions of her own dancing school (which were erratic because of the War). Toward the end of the War, during school holidays – when there was school – Julie was taken to whatever city her mother and stepfather were working in. Otherwise she stayed at home with a housekeeper.

'I enjoyed school,' she said, 'and like any other small girl I wanted to be just exactly the same as everyone else. No matter how hard Mummy tried to make this come true for me, I *was* different. I had two fathers, my parents were in show business, and I went to a different town each holiday-time. The girls I envied most were good at games; I was awful.'

But Julie kept practising, and developed such perfect pitch that thirty years later musicians would still marvel. 'I'm firmly convinced one can develop perfect pitch,' she said, 'you don't have to be born with it. I was one of those child-brat prodigies, and for my age I had an immensely powerful voice. It was to everyone's great surprise that it was there; there were no vocal musicians in my family.' (Those who didn't know that Ted Andrews was Julie's stepfather just assumed she had inherited her talent from him.)

In 1945, when Julie was ten, the War ended. The next year the Andrews family moved back to Walton-on-Thames and bought a house called The Old Meuse. Barbara Andrews later discovered that her mother had worked in that same house as a maid, and she herself continued to live there long after her only daughter became famous, and even after her second husband, Ted, died of a stroke in 1966. (The house was destroyed in 1973 to build a series of Old Meuse Townhouses.)

Julie continued to practise, and would sing for her friends, depending on her mood. 'Then came the day when I was told I must go to bed in the afternoon because I was going to be allowed to sing with Mummy and Pop in the evening,' she recalled. 'I had to stand on a beer crate to reach the microphone to sing my solo. It was such immense fun that I did it several times more, during school vacations, on an odd Tuesday night when it was not desperately important. My mother played the piano, my stepfather sang, and once in a while I joined him in a duet. It must have been ghastly, but it seemed to go down all right.'

Ted and Barbara Andrews would have to get permission

Singing at the *Starlight Roof* review 1947

from theatre managers for Julie to appear in these unbilled 'surprise bits' in their act. 'Some of the managers wouldn't take a chance on a rather ugly ten-year-old child,' Julie said. 'They thought my parents were quite out of their minds. But the ones that did take a chance were very nice.'

There had been some discussion of Julie's enrolling in the Royal Academy of Dramatic Art in London, but, as Barbara Andrews explained, 'we decided that a little toughening up as far as the theatre world was concerned would be good. So we took her into our act. Let's face it, it didn't hurt the act either.'

But after two years of Julie's occasional beer-box appearances with her parents, Ted Andrews decided that she was ready for a career of her own. Julie remembered herself at the age of twelve as a 'hideous child, with pigtails, crooked teeth, very bad legs' and two eyes that at times moved quite independently of each other. She had also inherited her mother's swooped nose and protruding jawline. But she also remembered her stepfather as 'a whizz at selling anything'.

One day in October 1947, just after Julie's twelfth birthday, Ted Andrews was playing golf with Val Parnell, the managing director of Moss Empires, the largest booking firm in England and owners of the London Palladium and Hippodrome, and theatres all over the provinces. Andrews persuaded Parnell to go home with him to hear Julie sing. Andrews went 'out to the garden and yanked this scruffy kid wearing a smudged smock into the house to sing an aria', the kid recalled. 'It was "I Am Titania" from *Mignon*.'

Parnell was impressed enough by her talent to sign Julie for a review, *Starlight Roof*, that was about to open at the Hippodrome. Instead of the aria he assigned her the much tamer 'Skater's Waltz'. But the night before the opening, 22 October, Parnell decided that the naïve girl singing the simple song wouldn't go with the rest of his sophisticated review (which starred Pat Kirkwood and comedians Fred Emney and Vic Oliver), and he fired her.

'My mother and my agent descended on him and said,

Playing in the Christmas panto *Little Red Riding Hood* in Nottingham 1949–50

"you've got to give this girl her big break", and all that sort of awful nonsense,' Julie remembered. Parnell did relent on the afternoon of the opening, but asked her to go back to Titania's aira from *Mignon*, 'a song ten times more difficult than the one I'd started out with'.

Fortunately, she knew the aria by heart, and that night she and the song were a success; the twelve-year-old reached F above high C with ease. Her routine involved sitting with her mother until it was time for her number. She went on stage, exchanged a few lines of dialogue with Vic Oliver, sang, and walked back down into the audience and out of the theatre without waiting to take a second curtain call at the end of the show. (Performers under the age of fifteen were prohibited by the London County Council from being in a theatre after 10.00 p.m.) Julie got all the notices the next day. 'I only had that one song,' she said, 'but fortunately it stopped the show.'

For this solo professional début Julie Andrews got £50 a

week, or rather her parents got it for her. All the girl got was a raise in her allowance from two to five shillings a week. The rest was supposed to go into a trust fund for her. Ted and Barbara Andrews turned down the first offer of a pantomime at £100 weekly, saying that they were determined that she be neither spoiled nor overworked. Val Parnell introduced Julie to Charles Tucker, 'Uncle Charlie', who became her manager and served in that capacity until 1965.

With Tucker in charge of her career 'the buck teeth were seen to immediately', and Julie settled into a year-long run at the Hippodrome, and non-stop work for the next twenty years, until she was well into her thirties, 'except for the odd holiday once in a while'.

There was little that could be done about Julie's bandy legs, but she corrected the eye defect by using the eye exercise developed by Dr William H. Bates. She felt she was getting by on her 'freak' singing. 'I knew no other profession, no other life; I didn't know that it was not good for a twelve-year-old girl to be singing in a sophisticated review. I just thought I was the luckiest girl alive.'

Julie had her first and only screen test that year she was twelve, at Metro-Goldwyn-Mayer in London, for the American producer Joseph Pasternak. 'They tried to make me look like a child star,' she recalled, 'but with my teeth and legs I didn't look like much of anything.' The screen test was made in black and white.

'Of course we never dreamed of film,' Barbara Andrews said on the set of *Little Miss Marker* in 1979. 'Julie used to complain bitterly about her nose and her jaw. But for a plain little girl I think she has some rare qualities, something that's not necessarily beauty, but a wonderfully warm quality that's somehow luminous.'

Starlight Roof did lead to Julie's being requested to appear at a Royal Command Variety Performance at the Palladium on 1 November 1948, a month to the day after her thirteenth birthday. Danny Kaye was the headliner, and Julie was

Princess Balroubadour in *Aladdin* in London 1951

described in the official announcement as 'a thirteen-year-old coloratura soprano with the voice of an adult'. She was the youngest solo performer ever chosen to perform for royalty at the Palladium. Queen Elizabeth, later to become the Queen Mother, was there with Princess Margaret. Julie again sang 'I Am Titania' from *Mignon*, on which 'I had nearly bust a gut taking a top F nightly for a year.' (She never missed that F during the run, but did sometimes later.)

'I was too excited for stage fright, and I got my notes out without mistakes,' she remembered, but when the Queen asked to meet Julie after the performance, 'my knees almost buckled; all I could think about was whether I should curtsy before and after meeting the Queen.'

'You sang beautifully, Julie, and we enjoyed it very much,' said Queen Elizabeth.

'I was in heaven,' said Julie.

Julie began to tour music halls all over Britain, sometimes with Ted and Barbara, but more often as a solo act, for which she was paid £75 a week. Either way, she figured, 'this was the daughter of Ted and Barbara Andrews that everyone had come to see. My mother and stepfather had become big stars, and I was in effect part of the act.' She followed them into radio and later into television. Julie's schooling, which had been sporadic at best, was abandoned entirely in favour of a governess and chaperone, who taught her for four hours a day for the next three years, until Julie was fifteen and stopped her formal learning altogether. 'I bitterly regret not having had more education,' she said.

Miss Knight (Julie never knew her first name) was the travelling tutor when Julie went 'on the halls'. After that, 'there was always someone like Alfred Marks or Max Wall to look after Julie,' Barbara Andrews remembered. But Julie always went home on Sundays, so her life was both rigorous and sheltered. Barbara Andrews did all the dealing with reporters, who mostly wanted to know 'How much money does little Julie make?' Even Julie didn't know the answer to that one until she was almost seventeen and firmly in the £150-weekly bracket.

'I had very little publicity,' Julie said, 'and applause was never to be overestimated. My mother helped me to keep a fairly level head, raising me strictly but fairly.

'It was good training for me and I suppose it paved the way for what was to come. I wouldn't change much if I could go back and do it all over. But I wouldn't raise my own children that way. Being in show business is unnatural for a child, and I'm not sure being an actor or actress, even as an adult, is the best thing in the world. Why are there so many performers going to psychiatrists? That should tell you something about the pressures and the problems.'

Julie toured Britain 'endlessly, it seems. It was lonely, and sometimes the towns were awfully bare and unpleasant. The worst things were Monday nights, Saturday night second house in a rough town like Glasgow, Cardiff or Liverpool, when you got all the rowdy people in and it was terrifying to stand up on stage. I didn't like it much, but it was good for me – a toughener-upper. Having survived the variety years, nothing else ever seemed so bad.'

Christmas pantomimes in London were much more fun than touring in vaudeville, which was 'on its last legs when I came on the scene. I mostly sang bastardized versions of operatic arias.' In 'pantos' however, 'I was always the principal girl who was rather wet and makes goo-goo eyes at Our Hero and gets him in the end.' She was Princess Balroulbadour in *Aladdin*, and played the title role in *Cinderella*. During *Humpty Dumpty* at the London Casino, when she was thirteen and playing the egg ('very Freudian'), Julie met Tony Walton, who was fourteen. On the train back to Walton-on-Thames, where Tony also lived, Tony and his three friends asked for autographs. 'He had seen the show, and we started talking,' Julie said. The next day he went to the theatre by himself and asked for photographs. 'He wrote me from school, and we became sort of mates. We saw each other at vacation times, whenever we could. That's the way it began, I guess.'

As Julie's career expanded, Ted and Barbara's began to slip. Julie was playing the best of the remaining vaudeville houses and her parents were playing the second best. One summer at the seaside resort of Blackpool, Barbara recalled, 'We were on the pier and she was at the big theatre in town – really a step above us.' Ted and Barbara played less and less frequently, and finally retired altogether. Julie, began to support the family (Ted and Barbara had two sons, Donald and Christopher), and even put one of her half-brothers through school.

'It's something we've never spoken of,' she said, 'but I can see now that it hurt terribly. If I hadn't been around, I suppose they'd have found a way to support themselves.'

'Weird and plenty seedy' was the way Tony Walton later described Julie's situation with her four dependents. 'From age thirteen on Julie was head of the family, and it was a grade-B movie existence. Right up until *Camelot* she had a guilt feeling about taking it easy.'

'She was an unhappy girl,' agreed Tancred Aegius, the boy next door in Walton-on-Thames, and Julie's boyfriend briefly when she was seventeen. 'Her mother and stepfather were always drunk – on liquor that she had paid for. It was sad.'

'As a young girl she bottled up her feelings, like the trooper she is,' said her real father, Ted Wells, 'and got on with the business of living. But then, nearly a quarter of a century later, all the pent-up unhappiness of that period suddenly caught up with her – so she sought the advice of a psychoanalyst.'

From her earliest years, to cover the truth of her home life, Julie wrote phoney diaries filled, in Tony's words, 'with fanciful images of what a beautiful, happy family life she had and what a glamorous existence she led'.

Ted Wells saved a story that Julie wrote when she was about five. It read as follows:

'Wuns the wos a mother and father. The motheer wanted a litl girl and boy. It was Crisms, the night Santer Claus hee cam to bring the two babis. Wen the mother woke up she was so pleased she loot for them and they live hapleevrovter.'

'To be truthful, at the time I think I thought I was happy,' Julie said. 'Children bounce back rather quickly from all their troubles. At any rate I would go around saying how desperately happy I was. I fancy I was protesting too much.'

Julie couldn't always decide whether she wanted to live with her mother or her father, but she knew she was 'precocious, a loner; I enjoyed the company of older people.' She spent a good deal of time with Ted Wells, both because she wanted to, and because he had had liberal visiting rights written into the custody agreement when he returned her to her mother. 'I guess I mostly wanted to be with my mother because she seemed to lead a rather colourful existence; she supplied the rougher, bawdier side of my life. My real father filled in the love of the countryside, outdoor sports, reading. When I was with him we led a quiet, more relaxed life. My stepmother was a wonderful woman, but I must admit I found it hard to live with my stepfather.'

Yet for public consumption, she idealized even Ted Andrews, and his and her mother's retirement. 'He has such a lovely voice; I'd rather listen to it than anything. Mummy always wanted to be just Mummy, so Pop gave up show business.'

Yet Ted Andrews and his stepdaughter shared a profession, one that in a very real sense he had given her. One night he took her to see *South Pacific* in the West End, 'the first big musical I'd ever seen. Pop said, "Just for one night we'll make it special." He put on a dinner jacket. Afterwards I talked about how wonderful the music was. My manager, Charles Tucker, said, "Some day, Julie, Rogers and Hammerstein will be writing songs for you."'

Work followed work and 'I couldn't think of anything else I could do or wanted to do.' Julie played in pantomimes and touring companies until she was eighteen. 'Most of the time I was kept in short, short dresses, patent-leather shoes and ankle socks, trying desperately to look ten years younger, growing a bosom and feeling wretched about that.'

At seventeen Julie played Cinderella at the Palladium; Max Bygraves played Buttons. At eighteen she played a Southern belle from Tennessee in a play with music, called *Mountain Fire*, in Leeds, Yorkshire. 'It was an incredible disaster,' she recalled. 'The story was all about Sodom and Gomorrah and bootleg whisky and Lot's wife turning to a pillar of salt. I can't tell you what went on. You've never heard a worse Southern accent than mine. In the play I got pregnant by a travelling salesman. Thank God the miserable thing closed before we got to London.'

Both *Cinderella* and *Mountain Fire* were responsible for sending Julie to America, where she 'heard a real Southern accent and nearly died of shame'. But in 1953, Julie Andrews wasn't thinking about the United States or even of an acting career in England. 'All the time I was growing up I knew I could sing,' she said, 'and I thought that was rather good. But I didn't ever dream I would be singing after my childhood. I used to think: "What am I going to do when I grow up?"'

2

AMERICA AND
THE BOY FRIEND

THE BOY FRIEND, Sandy Wilson's affectionate lampoon of the 1920s, became a home-grown musical hit in London's West End in 1954, and was bought by producers Cy Feuer and Ernie Martin for a Broadway opening that September. It was still too early in the London run to transfer any of the original cast to America, but Feuer and Martin, Wilson, and director Vida Hope and choreographer John Heawood were determined to retain the flavour of the West End original, and they agreed that meant casting all-English leads. Anne Rogers had scored a personal triumph in the leading role of sweet Polly Browne, and the major problem was replacing her for what they all expected to be an extended New York run.

Vida Hope had seen Julie's Cinderella the previous Christmas, and Sandy Wilson remembered her *Starlight Roof* appearance six years earlier, when 'still a small girl in a party frock and large white shoes, she had filled the theatre with a soprano of astonishing range and purity.' Hope and Feuer took a train to Leeds to catch Julie in *Mountain Fire*. The producer was horrified by her dialect, and by her breaking off her dialogue to begin a song, *after* which the leading man and the orchestra came in, but found 'her pitch was perfect and her voice was delightful.'

Julie was invited to audition for *The Boy Friend* at the London Coliseum. Wilson remembered that her mother Barbara, 'a rather forceful lady with red hair, came with her and sat in the pit to accompany her'. Heawood, the choreographer, called it 'pure *Gypsy*. We asked her to dance and Barbara stood up and said, "Go on Julie, show them your tap." Julie, being very modest, said, "I don't think I can." But she did, and at the end of this very difficult audition, Vida whispered to me, "That's it. We've found her."'

Ted and Barbara, and Charles Tucker, were all for Julie's doing Polly Browne on Broadway, but her first thought was, 'Oh, good Christ, the idea of leaving my home and family – I couldn't do it. I had toured on my own all through England, but suddenly the idea of two years in America was too much.' I did what I always did when I had a tough decision to make: I asked my Dad, my real Dad, the wisest and dearest man I knew. He advised me to see America while I had the chance, and he pointed out that the show might not be a hit and might last only a very short time. I decided to go if I could get them to agree to a one-year contract. It was the first time I really put my foot down on something. I wouldn't have earned enough to bring my family over, and they certainly couldn't afford it, so one year was it.'

'Her parents had to sign her over to us because of her age,' Feuer remembered, 'but I was struck by her maturity. Most performers at that age are very amateurish, but even then she had great equanimity and poise. She didn't rattle. She had a very good dramatic ability even then; she was an instinctive actress.'

Before the *Boy Friend* troupe left for America, Wilson took his new leading lady out to dinner. With Vida Hope and her husband, and Neil McCallum, an actor and Julie's current

Julie's first Broadway appearance, as Polly Browne in *The Boy Friend* during the 'Poor Little Pierrette' number 1954 NEW YORK TIMES

admirer, they went to the Royal Court Theatre Club, then a restaurant-cabaret. 'Throughout the evening I was struck again by Julie's perfect behaviour: a combination of school-girlish innocence and a control and poise far in advance of her years,' Wilson wrote in his autobiography *I Could Be Happy*. 'As I watched her and listened to her, I wondered if we might be about to assist at the birth of a new star, someone as remarkable in her way as Gertrude Lawrence. Then, in a moment of insight unusual for me, I realized that this girl would be a star anyway, with or without our assistance. It was nothing that she said or did, and she certainly betrayed no symptoms of egotism or ambition; she simply had about her an unmistakable air of cool, clear-cut determination. For Julie, I could tell, it was going to be the top or nothing.'

Julie arrived in New York in August 1954, 'during an immense heat-wave'. Her first home was the seedy Piccadilly Hotel on West 45th Street, near Broadway. Only its name was English. 'I had one room with a tiny window,' she recall-ed. Even for someone who had known early poverty and tacky English music halls, that was hardly adequate, so Julie and Dilys Lay, who played Dulcie in *The Boy Friend*, agreed to share an apartment. Julie termed it 'a modest suite in the modest Park Chambers Hotel on Sixth Avenue (which, down at our end, near Central Park, you might call New York's Bloomsbury)'. It had a bedroom, living room and a stand-up kitchenette. The rent, $275 a month – payable in advance, was anything but modest for the West Side of New York in the mid-1950s.

'It made a horrible hole in our budget,' Julie said, 'and I had no sense of money or of taking care of myself.' The girls had to get an advance on their $100-weekly rehearsal salaries to get into the apartment, and almost two-thirds of Julie's $400-a-week salary during the actual run of the show went for taxes, Charles Tucker, and family support. Much of the rest went on trans-Atlantic phone calls back to Walton-on-Thames, during which Julie's half-brother Donald would kick her Welsh

Corgi Hump (short for Humpty) to get him to bark into the telephone.

At the rooms in 'Bloomsbury', Dilys did the cooking, while Julie did the shopping, 'the washing up and made endless pots of tea'. To make the suite more habitable the girls hung red paper bells from the ceiling. They bought an electric broiler to learn to cook American-style, and a dachshund named Melanie, which they gave to each other for Christmas.

At first Julie didn't like New York: 'too large, too humid, too noisy, too crowded, too expensive. I was frightened of it.' There were the 'soggy tea-bags and ghastly water', but there were also '"poppets": the New York cab drivers; the second teller from the left at Manufacturers Trust Company; and other people you love in spite of everything.' Julie also liked Dixieland, the East Side of Manhattan, Benny Goodman, Johnny Ray and Frank Sinatra, the Latin Quarter, the Stork Club and '21'. She loved American drugstores, so much more comprehensive than English chemists; 'cream cheese and jelly, sandwiches, your wonderful milk shakes – ruinous but marvellous, and your beer, fine for me, light, as the commercials say, but I'm afraid an Englishman wouldn't like it.'

The girls found differences between English and American men, besides their taste in beer.

'A British friend asks you where you would like to go,' said Julie, 'but an American says you're going *here* or *there*.'

'Usually both,' said Dilys, 'with Americans one does get around a bit.'

Professionally, things weren't quite so cosy or so much fun. Because a totally new company had been created for *The Boy Friend* on Broadway, there were six weeks of rehearsals and previews before the show opened on the last day of September. The hours were frequently from 10.00 a.m. through to 4.00 the next morning, 'and not a minute is wasted,' Julie wrote home. 'It's detail, detail all the way. Every gesture, every line, is gone over, again and again. But it's fun and terrific experience. If I miss anything at all, it's not backstage but at the front of the house. Theatres here haven't got the regal atmosphere and character that they have in London. You get the impression the people who designed them had only one idea: to pack in as many customers as possible.'

The original production of *The Boy Friend* at Wyndham's Theatre in the West End had cost about £2,000; the New York version was costing £60,000, and, despite the producers' protestations of fidelity to the original (they had filmed a London performance in order to copy the costumes, scenery and props down to the minutest detail), what had been an intimate show was being transformed into a big Broadway musical. Cast members were fired, replaced and rearranged; Feuer and Martin even fired Vida Hope as director (though her name remained on the credits), and Feuer took over himself. Sandy Wilson was barred, along with Hope, from the theatre until opening night. A number crucial to the delicate structure of the story (a rich girl at a private school on the Riviera falls in love with a messenger boy who turns out to be as rich as she) was cut. 'It's Nicer in Nice' reappeared in most revivals of *The Boy Friend* but wasn't heard on Broadway.

Julie survived the turmoil, although John Heawood, the choreographer (who also survived), recalled that at one point 'they wanted the understudy to replace her; she was a woman of about thirty-five, who sang very nicely and moved like a Churchill tank.'

'I was awful,' Julie recalled, 'I had to learn a whole new style of acting for this show – my own style was rather quiet.' One day during previews Feuer took Julie out by the theatre's fire escape. 'He sat me down and said: "You were simply lousy last night. You're trying to be clever and it's dead. You're way, way out and sending it up rotten." He really let me have it. He said, "Believe everything you say – *be* Polly. If you do that, you'll be a success. If you don't, you'll be a disaster." Thanks to Cy and his advice I *was* Polly. I did it because I was told to do it.'

Feuer insisted that he 'couldn't teach Julie very much.

Before leaving Britain for America 1954

Dramatically she had it all along. She performed far beyond the ability of anyone that age. She was a marvellous person to work with, a very sweet person. She did everything you asked without complaint, and was a lot of fun. There's some kind of bubble inside her. She was just everything you could ask for in a performer, and always on time.'

Opening night at the Royale Theatre found most critics enthralled with the show and with Julie as Polly Browne. The *New York Times* drama critic Brooks Atkinson, then the doyen of 'the Seven Butchers of Broadway', called *The Boy Friend* 'a delightful burlesque . . . extremely well done in manuscript as well as on stage. [Wilson] has written book, songs and lyrics with satirical inventiveness; and someone has directed it with great ironic skill. It is hard to say which is funnier: the material or the performance.'

Atkinson called Dilys Lay as Dulcie 'a miniature Beatrice Lillie', but wrote, 'It is probably Julie Andrews, as the heroine, who gives *The Boy Friend* its special quality. She burlesques the insipidity of the part. She keeps the romance very sad. Her hesitating gestures and her wistful shy mannerisms are very comic.'

Only Henry Hewes, writing in the *Saturday Review*, dissented. 'What Feuer and Martin have done to this show is make a fast, raucous burlesque out of a carefree valentine, [but] very possibly only those looking for an old sweetheart will find *The Boy Friend* a loud-mouthed date who, unlike his British cousin, *knows* he is being the life of the party.'

At the box office *The Boy Friend* was an unqualified hit, beginning the next morning, 1 October 1954, Julie's nineteenth birthday. She celebrated with a breakfast of bacon and eggs in bed, and wrote a ten-page letter to her mother about the opening-night triumph. Barbara Andrews soon flew over to New York to share that success, leaving behind in Walton-on-Thames the stepfather who had insisted on Julie's singing lessons, 'to break the barrier between us. But of course that was rather like a husband teaching his wife to drive: it only increased the tension.'

Nonetheless, Julie's delivery of such songs as 'I Could Be Happy with You', 'A Room in Bloomsbury', 'Poor Little Pierette', and the title song, 'The Boy Friend', more than justified Ted Andrews' long-standing faith in her talent. She was given feature-billing in November, the only member of either the London or New York cast so honoured, and the following April, in 1955, Julie returned from Ebbets Field in Brooklyn, and her first American baseball game, to find that she (along with John Hewer, who played the messenger boy) had been promoted even further, to above-the-title star.

Feuer explained Julie's success in *The Boy Friend* as the result of a combination of attributes, only one of which was her voice. 'This girl is tall, she has large features – which are great for the stage: you can see her a mile away. People like that take light. They don't disappear into the scenery. Taken singly, those features may not be much, but the way they're put together, they turn out to be attractive. She is a kind of built-in leading lady, has a kind of built-in dignity and a kind of built-in musical know-how.'

Julie pronounced herself 'thrilled' with the recognition, but remained somewhat reticent. 'Here you make a star out of practically nothing too quickly,' she said. 'In England you have to prove yourself over a long period in a variety of roles. In England I wouldn't be considered to have arrived yet. We adopt more of a wait-and-see attitude there. Here, one has one hit and, whoosh! Well, I'm English and I'm waiting and seeing.'

She didn't have to wait very long. In less than eighteen months Julie would be playing a role with which she would still be indelibly identified twenty-five years later: Eliza Doolittle. 'I realize now,' said Julie after the release of her first four movies, 'that the high point in my life was coming to America. I was very aware, even at the time, of having some door open somewhere and passing through it. I was on my own, and standing on my own two feet for the first time. I was having to function as an independent person, where before I'd been a guarded child.'

39

3

BROADWAY'S FAIR LADY

In April 1955, slightly, past the mid-point of her year in *The Boy Friend*, Julie got a call from a representative of Alan Jay Lerner and Frederick Loewe, routinely asking when she would be available again. She had been suggested for a musical version of George Bernard Shaw's *Pygmalion* that Lerner and Loewe were doing. 'When I told him I would be free in August he almost fell off the other end of the phone,' she remembered, 'they had assumed I had a two-year contract like everyone else. Because I thought I'd get homesick, I was free at just the right time.'

Julie auditioned for Lerner, the lyricist-adaptor, and Loewe, the composer, and was offered the role of Eliza. She had also auditioned for Richard Rodgers, who was casting *Pipe Dream*, but 'Dick was absolutely wonderful about it and said *Pygmalion* would be the wiser move,' said Julie. 'Until *My Fair Lady* I hadn't done anything for any reason except that I was told to; it was my job. But the year I spent in *The Boy Friend* was one of the best of my life, and I learned a lot

41

about timing and comedy from American audiences. I used to be a slow learner, and it was a marvellous experience to learn on the job and get away with it.'

Learning on the job was to be an important part of *My Fair Lady* for Julie, too, but first there was a five-month holiday at home in Walton-on-Thames, lasting through Christmas (except for a week in Hollywood to do *High Tor* for television). 'I had given her a copy of the play to think about over the vacation,' recalled Alan Jay Lerner, 'and told her we would see when rehearsals began. Her first try-outs had not been very good. Julie had no sense of being a star, none of that sense of obligation that a star has toward a play. The others, Rex Harrison [Professor Henry Higgins] and Stanley Holloway [Alfred Doolittle], turned up several weeks ahead to talk over their parts. Not Julie. She sent us a letter saying she would arrive from London on the day rehearsals began, not before, because she had promised to take her two little brothers to a pantomime. It was so different, so unbelievably unprofessional, that we were amused rather than annoyed.'

Another reason for Julie's delay might have been sheer terror. The twenty-year-old actress regarded this musical as 'a monstrous task. Shaw simply terrified me. The singing part was the only thing I thought I might somehow do. When it came to acting, I was simply awful at first, and terrified of Rex Harrison. It was obvious that I needed a lot of attention.'

Shaw had described Eliza Doolittle, in his stage directions, as 'perhaps eighteen, perhaps twenty, hardly older'. Lerner's book had kept that conception. Yet Julie was the first actress of that age to play the part. Mrs Patrick Campbell, for whom Shaw originally wrote the play, was forty-nine when she appeared in *Pygmalion* in London, in 1914. Lynn Fontanne was thirty-nine when she played Eliza for the Theatre Guild in New York in 1926. Gertrude Lawrence was forty-four when she played the cockney flower-girl on Broadway in 1945. Even Wendy Hiller, the definitive Eliza so far as *My Fair Lady* was concerned (both Lerner and Andrews ran the

My Fair Lady 1956 FRIEDMAN-ABELES, NEW YORK

motion picture *Pygmalion* many times over), was twenty-six when the movie was released in 1938. And Julie Harris was well into her thirties when she did Eliza on television.

At the start of rehearsals, on 3 January 1956, Julie's age and singing voice were all that were right. Rex Harrison recalled her 'defiant nervousness', and was annoyed when she loudly practised her scales in the theatre. 'I wouldn't be surprised if there hadn't been times when they all thought of sending me back to London,' Julie said.

Moss Hart, *My Fair Lady*'s director, met Julie for the first time at rehearsal, and recalled that she 'was charming but didn't have a clue about playing Eliza. About the fifth day I got really terrified that she was not going to make it.' Julie told friends that she thought she knew what Hart wanted, but that every time she tried to do it, 'something comes up in front of me and I'm like a crab clawing at a glass wall with Moss on the other side.' Hart cancelled general rehearsals for a weekend and spent two days alone with Julie trying to develop her performance.

She called it 'the now-famous, dreaded weekend', and he termed it 'the days of terror. It was the sort of thing you couldn't do in front of a company without destroying a human being. We met in this silent, lonely, dark theatre, and I told her, "This is stolen time, time I can't really afford. So there can be no time for politeness, and you mustn't take offence, because there aren't any second chances in the theatre. There isn't time to do the whole Actors' Studio bit. We have to start from the first line and go over the play line by line." With someone not gifted, this would have meant nothing, this rehearsal in depth.'

'He was like a Svengali,' she recalled, 'he bullied and pleaded, coaxed and cajoled. He said, "You're playing this like a girl guide," "You're not *thinking*, you're just oozing out the scene," or "You're gabbling." He made me *be* Eliza.'

'Those two days made the difference,' Hart agreed. 'She was neither affronted nor hurt. She was delighted. We were

As Eliza Doolittle, with Rex Harrison as Professor Higgins in
My Fair Lady 1956 FRIEDMAN-ABELES, NEW YORK

both absolutely exhausted, but she made it. She has that terrible English strength that makes you wonder why they lost India.'

'He made me infuriated, and scared and mad and frightened and in awe and full of an inferiority complex,' she admitted years later, 'while knowing I could do it, he worked and worked on me. I really did need a strong guiding hand. It was such a big musical and I had so little courage. I didn't know what Eliza should be, a whiny girl or a gutsy girl, a weak character or a strong one. Moss supplied the route, and as the nights went by, I absorbed Eliza more and more.'

Frequently Julie and her Svengali would have fifteen-minute refresher sessions in the powder room at the Mark Hellinger Theatre, while the rest of the cast continued rehearsals on stage. For the next three and half years (two on Broadway, eighteen months in London) Julie 'was never really sure, on any given night, that I had enough strength to do the whole thing flat out. I found it an enormous weight every night and I can't remember a single performance when I didn't wonder to myself: "Am I going to get through it tonight?" and "I'll have to save myself a little in this song so that I have enough voice left for my next number." It was such an enormous show – the screaming, the singing purely, the singing "on the chest", the great dramatic requirements.'

Rex Harrison remembered that it was difficult at first for Julie to do the long Shaw dialogue scenes. 'The other thing that she found difficult,' he said, 'and Audrey [Hepburn, in the movie version of *My Fair Lady*] did too, was to get the gutter quality in Liza – that's a very exacting thing.'

Julie took great delight in the fact that she learned her cockney from an American, Alfred Dixon, a former actor who had been teaching pronunciation for twenty-five years. Dixon had catalogued, he said, all the world's inflections of speech, and he was as close a vocational cousin to Henry Higgins as could be found. At first the cockney used in *My Fair Lady* was too authentic for American audiences and had to be toned down considerably. 'The trouble with the dialect,' Julie recalled, 'was that it varied slightly between men and women, and between that in use today and in the period of the play, which is Edwardian. In those days men were different: their voices were deep and low, and the women's were shriller and sort of high.'

Unlike most musical comedy hits that are formed over a long period of trying out, rewriting and reworking, *My Fair Lady* was a winner almost from the first, Julie's performing problems notwithstanding. The creators and cast had total confidence in the property and were not tempted to make major changes. Lerner had been faithful to the spirit of Shaw's play (though he had appropriated the movie's more upbeat ending), and it was nearly impossible to tell where he had invented new scenes and dialogue. Loewe's score and Lerner's lyrics all soared on first hearing. Julie, who sang no fewer than eight of the show's songs – including 'I Could Have Danced All Night', 'Wouldn't It Be Loverly', 'Show Me' and 'Without You' – 'aged ten years on the road', according to Lerner. The rest of the English principals, including Holloway, Robert Coote as Colonel Pickering, Harrison and Cathleen Nesbitt as Mrs Higgins (the two latter playing son and mother in the 1981–2 revival of *My Fair Lady* as well, in their seventies and nineties respectively), were calm enough to take their tea-breaks every day at four during rehearsals.

By the time the out-of-town try-outs took place in New Haven and Philadelphia, in February and early March, the word was out that *My Fair Lady* was the next big hit, and Julie Andrews was the next big Broadway star. There were so many requests for New York opening-night tickets during the last two weeks in Philadelphia that Andrews and Harrison both refused to take long-distance telephone calls at their hotel.

Barbara Andrews was among the glittering première audience at the Hellinger on 15 March 1956. 'Opening night of *My Fair Lady* in New York was the greatest night of my life,'

Singing 'The Rain in Spain' with Robert Coote and Rex Harrison
in *My Fair Lady* 1956 FRIEDMAN-ABELES, NEW YORK

Mrs Andrews declared. 'Apart from the night I had Julie. That first transformation from the guttersnipe Eliza to her appearance at the Ascot races! And the ball scene, when she came down in white, with the feather!' Barbara Andrews was quite justifiably proud of her daughter's performance, and tumultuous ovations after every song were a testament to Julie's success.

The critics concurred. Walter Kerr, in the New York *Herald Tribune*, wrote: 'Miss Andrews descended a staircase looking like all the glamour of the theatre summed up in an instant.' Brooks Atkinson in the *New York Times* called the show 'wonderful . . . To Shaw's agile intelligence it adds the warmth, loveliness and excitement of a memorable theatre frolic.' Julie, he said, 'does a magnificent job. The transformation from street-corner drab to lady is both touching and beautiful. Miss Andrews acts her part triumphantly.'

A line began to form at the Mark Hellinger box office the day after the opening, and for the next eight years *My Fair Lady* shattered all Broadway attendance and revenue records. (There were to be longer runs in the 1970s, *Hello, Dolly!*, *Fiddler on the Roof* and *Grease* each breaking its predecessor's record). The show was completely sold out every night of the two years that Andrews and Harrison were in it. The original cast album outgrossed the show, with one million copies and $5 million in the first year of its release; *My Fair Lady* became and remained the best-selling original Broadway cast album of all time. The sale of the movie rights to Warner Brothers was for $5 million, a price unsurpassed twenty-five years later. An American touring company, the London production and various foreign language versions of *My Fair Lady* brought the property's gross receipts to something over $100 million.

Only two months before, in rehearsals, Julie had burst out laughing at every serious scene Rex Harrison played. 'It was a form of nerves, I think,' he said. 'She was really only a kid and it must have been a frightening experience for her – I always asked her why she laughed and she never did tell me.' She was now inundated with offers to better her already respectable $2,000-a-week salary. She became the first international leading lady since Gertrude Lawrence had arrived in New York in 1924 and sang 'Limehouse Blues' in *Charlot's Revue*.

'Toast of the town,' she said with some sarcasm. 'I haven't had time to be toasted very much . . . I receive a great many invitations, but I can accept only a few. I dare not go out before a matinée, and the next day I am recuperating from two shows. People expect so much more of you after something like this – more letters, more effort, more entrances. Then if you don't produce, they think you've gone big-headed.'

Julie had moved back into the modest suite at the Park Chambers, by herself this time. It was the first time she had lived alone, and she pronounced it 'not so terrifying as I had imagined'. Shortly after *My Fair Lady* opened, she moved to 'a minute flat in the East Sixties with a sweet little patio in back and a proper cooking range'. Mornings she slept until 11.00 a.m. or 12.00 noon, trying to rest nine and a half hours a night. She rented studio space to practise her singing an hour a day, and eschewed the cheeseburgers she had come to love, in order to keep her flower-girl figure.

Homesick for the English spring, she bought daffodils from the flower man outside her subway stop, as a pale reminder of the clumps outside her window in Walton-on-Thames. She sent Dictaphone 'letters' back home every week, and found that the best thing about her new affluence was that she could afford to fly family members to New York for visits. Julie decided that in any future career she would live in England and spend three or four months of the year in the United States working, preferably in American autumn. But she preferred her homeland because 'I like the smallness of England; it's all so vast over here, it really knocks you off your feet.'

Tony Walton arrived in New York in April 1956, just a

month after the opening of *My Fair Lady*, to study scenic design. Julie spent much of her free time with him, and he called for her at the theatre after every performance. They picnicked in the country whenever possible, and took an out-of-season winter vacation in Bear Mountain, New York (after turning down invitations to Nassau, Jamaica and Bermuda), in 1957, during a week off from *My Fair Lady*. On many nights, after the show, they went to the Windsor pharmacy at 58th Street and Sixth Avenue for a 'Windsor Special', which Julie described as 'a banana thing with wads of coconut cream'.

Denying that she and Tony were engaged (as her mother and stepfather were having to do in England), Julie nevertheless publicly acknowledged him as her boyfriend. For her twenty-first birthday, 1 October 1956, he gave her a brooch in the shape of a laurel wreath that she wore on everything. The future course of the romance had been decided, but they were putting off a formal engagement because Julie had to do Eliza in London after Broadway, and Tony had to take his examinations for the scenic design union in New York. Julie depended on Tony to be another Svengali. 'She has no conception of her capabilities,' he said. 'It's all there – just needs a bit of dragging out.'

Charles Tucker gave Julie her first furs for her twenty-first birthday, a black sealskin coat with which to combat New York winter. But now that, as a Broadway star, she could afford just about anything she wanted, Julie seemed to have lost a good deal of her former acquisitiveness. 'Every time I'm tempted by something elaborate,' she said, 'I hear Mummy saying: "Simplicity, simplicity."'

Though intermittently insecure ('I still feel unsure sometimes, as though I've tackled something miles above me'), Julie was no longer a problem child for the cast and management of *My Fair Lady*. Moss Hart said she reminded him of Gertrude Lawrence, whom he had directed in *Lady in the Dark*, and he added: 'She has this curious kind of glacial calm,

My Fair Lady 1956 FRIEDMAN-ABELES, NEW YORK

as though she came down from Everest every day to play the show, instead of from a hotel room.' Stanley Holloway said, 'This child isn't spoiled one bit by success – it's hardly believable in an age where teenagers are so worldly. I'm lucky to have her for a stage daughter. She *might* have been a scene-stealer.'

Even Rex Harrison, who used to amuse himself trying to rattle her by changing around bits of stage business, finally gave into her surface calm. (The rest of the cast called her the Rock because she'd stand stoically by while Rex pulled his pranks.) 'She is absolutely the same off-stage as on,' Harrison said. 'She is marvellously even, her performance doesn't vary; it is highly professional from the word "go". Julie was always – a very boring old word – a good trouper. She ploughed on through thick and thin. One thousand performances over three years is three thousand hours – four months and five days of twenty-four hours a day. I had my secretary figure it out. That is quite a hell of a long time to have been vis-à-vis with somebody, through summers hot, winters cold, that sort of thing. She has an honesty and integrity, an openness, a quality of the English equivalent of the girl next door. She reminds me of some of the English ladies at Metro [Goldwyn-Mayer]: Greer [Garson] and Deborah [Kerr]. She is not quite the same as they, but she has that very same quality that has appealed to movie audiences over the years.'

But Julie wasn't thinking of movies in 1956, except to attend them occasionally. (She and Tony accepted, as one of the 'perks' of her new stardom, reserved seats to the sold-out *Around the World in Eighty Days*). In fact, she had no show-business aspirations beyond *My Fair Lady*, she said. 'I'd like to work awfully hard for another two years, then marry, then have lots of children. I really wouldn't mind retiring, or working in London on one thing a year. I haven't much desire to go on to bigger and better things – what could be bigger and better than this?'

4

CINDERELLA MARRIES HER PRINCE

JUST five nights before *My Fair Lady* opened in New York, Julie made her American television début with a filmed musical version of Maxwell Anderson's *High Tor* on CBS TV. The show had been filmed in Hollywood the previous November, 1955, during her long vacation after *The Boy Friend*, because she and co-star, Bing Crosby, were available then. It took every bit of the four months until it aired to cut and score the film, which was CBS's first non-live entertainment special.

Crosby played the lead role of a contemporary young idealist, Van Van Dorn, who owned the historic High Tor mountain in the Dutch-settled section of lower New York State. He loved the ghost of a Dutch girl, Lise, dead for three hundred years, and played by Andrews. Nancy Olson played Van Dorn's real-life fiancée. Arthur Schwartz, who also produced the show, wrote six songs, for which Anderson wrote the lyrics. CBS spent $300,000, then a record for a television show, much of it to recreate in plaster the mist-wrapped, craggy mountain at RKO-Pathe Studio in Hollywood (although a second-unit crew went East and climbed High Tor for some authentic long shots). The total shooting schedule was twelve days.

The key premise of both the original play, and this musical version, which Anderson himself adapted, was that the love between Van Dorn and Lise, across three centuries, was doomed. It was summed up in one scene between Andrews and Crosby, where they looked dreamily over what was supposed to be Long Island Sound at the stars. 'See the great gulf that lies between the heavy red star down in the west and the star that comes with the morning?' Lise asked. 'There's that much lies between us.'

Despite the fact that Bing Crosby starred in *High Tor*, this first appearance before movie cameras was not a distinguished one for Julie. The big singing part had been his, and he had been wrong for it. The static 'special' looked like the studio set quickie that it was, and the scene between the man of the 1950s and the girl of the 1650s lacked feeling. Still, it gave Julie her first trip to Hollywood.

She had better luck the next year, 1957, with the title part in *Cinderella*, the only full-length original work done for television by Richard Rodgers and Oscar Hammerstein II. By then, Julie had been established as Eliza Doolittle, a kind of Cinderella character, for over a year. Hammerstein had adapted the fairy tale for the ninety-minute musical version, with the principal change that the wicked stepmother (Ilka Chase) and stepsisters (Kay Ballard and Alice Ghostley) were less wicked and more comically vaudevillian. Edie Adams played the fairy godmother, Jon Cypher was the Prince, and Howard Lindsey and Dorothy Stickney were the King and Queen. Ralph Nelson directed the special, one of the first transmitted in colour, at a time when only a tiny percentage of Americans had access to a colour television set. One critic said that Julie as Cinderella was 'the best reason yet' to buy one.

With Rodgers and Hammerstein songs such as 'Ten

In her first American television special, *High Tor,* with Bing Crosby
1955 CULVER PICTURES

As Cinderella in the Rogers and Hammerstein televised version,
with Alice Ghostley and Kaye Ballard as the stepsisters and
Ilka Chase as the stepmother 1947 CBS TELEVISION

Minutes Ago', 'In My Little Corner', 'Lovely Night', and especially 'Do I Love You Because You're Beautiful? (Or Are You Beautiful Because I Love You?)', the musical *Cinderella* was a charming and unforgettable television event. Julie and the rest of the cast were at their best, and the show should have become a much-repeated TV classic, instead of being re-made in 1964 with the same score but with Lesley Ann Warren in the title role, and a lesser supporting cast.

In the spring of 1958, Julie played Eliza Doolittle on Broadway for the last time, then went on holiday with Tony Walton to Paris, Venice and Klosters, Switzerland. She flew into London on 6 April, deliberately cutting it close to her West End opening in *My Fair Lady* on 30 April. (Her New York success had made her comparatively wealthy and arriving home any sooner would have made her liable for British income tax on her American income, a situation that was to keep her away from England for most of the next twenty-five years.) The girl who had flown to New York nearly four years before with two battered, vaudeville-seasoned suitcases, arrived with 260 pounds of excess baggage – and a canary, Mr Pocket (after the Alec Guinness character in the film *Great Expectations*), a parting gift from the *My Fair Lady* cast. Seven more trunks were on their way from America.

Julie wore the sealskin coat Charles Tucker had given her, a clinging American-designed white wool dress, a seed-pearl-and-gold locket (another gift from the *My Fair Lady* cast) and a pearl-and-gold ring from Tony on her right hand. Her father Ted Wells, her brother John and half-sister Celia, and a score of friends met the plane from Zurich. Tony had stayed behind in Switzerland, but returned to London in time for the opening night. Julie went home to Walton-on-Thames for one night, then moved to a suite at the Savoy Hotel for the start of rehearsals.

Harrison and Holloway were also returning home for the West End production of *My Fair Lady* at the Theatre Royal,

hard by Covent Garden, where two of the major scenes in the musical are set. This theatre has a larger stage than the Mark Hellinger (although a smaller seating capacity), and eight singers were added to the chorus. Zena Dare made the final appearance of her long and distinguished career, as Mrs Higgins. Julie's major problem was to 'brush up on my cockney and put back the heavy accent that I had had to tone down.'

Tickets proved every bit as hard to get for *My Fair Lady* in London as they had been in New York, and there was a general air of high expectation unusual for the importation of an American musical to the West End. To some extent, of course, it was an 'English' musical in content (and Britons Sally Ann Howes and Edward Mulhare had replaced Andrews and Harrison on Broadway), and opening night in its spiritual home proved triumphant.

Most of the white-tie opening-night audience came away agreeing that the musical was indeed as good as the Yanks had promised it would be. There was a four-minute standing ovation at the final curtain, and eight curtain calls; there would have been more, but the conductor broke into 'God Save the Queen'. Critics were generally fulsome, and those who had seen the show in New York as well felt the musical had had a beneficial sea change. The leading lady who had sung in *Starlight Roof* in pigtails a scant ten years before was praised as generously as the show. One critic found Julie's West End Eliza 'more mature, commanding and subtle' than her Broadway performance.

A little more than a year later, on 10 May 1959, during a three-week vacation from *My Fair Lady*, Julie Andrews married Tony Walton at St Mary's village church of Oatlands, Weybridge, Surrey. Two thousand fans turned up outside the church. Julie wore a white organza silk dress that Tony had designed. Noel Harrison, who was the somewhat estranged son of Rex, and who had been at school with Tony, served as best man. The reception was held at the Mitre, a 300-year-old

inn opposite Hampton Court Palace on the bank of the Thames. The wedding trip took the couple to California, where the 23-year-old bride had to tape a television special.

The day before the wedding Julie spent at her apartment on Eaton Square (where she had moved from the Savoy), in a cotton housecoat, accepting delivery of wedding presents. The afternoon was divided between her dressmaker, a theatrical costumer in Soho (Tony waited outside – he may have designed the wedding dress, but he wasn't going to see her in it before the ceremony), and her mother's house in the country, where she planned the flowers. She had a late-afternoon sitting for a portrait with Pietro Annigoni, and dinner with her business manager. Typically, she stayed up late, writing thank-you notes.

Julie's engagement to Tony, she recalled, had 'just evolved. I don't remember one glorious night on bended knee. We were – here's the cliché – just good friends for a very long time, and then it grew into love. I guess you could say we were childhood sweethearts, and I'm very glad we were. On the day we got married I was glad I had known him so long. It's a big step to take, and it's better to do it with someone you know that well.'

On 8 August 1959, Julie played Eliza Doolittle for the last time. She confessed to being 'tired-tired, but not bored-tired, of being part of a legend. You don't want to go on,' she said, 'but suddenly you don't want to go, either. The old firm, the old job, becomes very dear.'

Thus, when she took her applause for more than the thousandth time on her closing night in *My Fair Lady*, tears rolled in rivers through her stage make-up. The audience joined hands and sang 'Auld Lang Syne', then the cast gave Julie an ovation. She ran to her dressing room, where she stayed for more than an hour, crying, but later hosted a party at the theatre. The next night her role of Eliza was taken over by Anne Rogers, from whom Julie had inherited the role of

Polly in *The Boy Friend.*

After a total of three and a half years in *My Fair Lady*, Julie found her voice 'was in a ragged state from night after night of belting. Then I had my tonsils out – at age twenty-three. I thought I would never sing again. It was an enormous period of anxiety about my voice. I very tentatively and timidly took on *Camelot*. The next eighteen months were a miracle to me – I got my voice back.'

Camelot had started to come about in early March of 1956, when it was apparent that *My Fair Lady* would be a hit. Lerner, Loewe and Hart took an informal pledge to work together again on a musical and they began to look for an idea. They considered and rejected musicals based on *Huckleberry Finn* and *Father of the Bride*, the Spencer Tracy–Elizabeth Taylor movie, but were intrigued by the book *The Once and Future King*, T. H. White's witty retelling of the King Arthur, Guinevere and Lancelot legend. The trio bought the stage rights from White, who was then living on the Channel Island of Alderney. The musical was completed in July 1960, and rehearsals began in September, under the title of *Jenny Kissed Me.*

'We all believed in the book immensely, and thought it would be a very beautiful musical,' Julie recalled. Because she and the *My Fair Lady* creative team were involved, great things were expected of *Jenny Kissed Me*. Richard Burton had been signed to make his musical début, which contributed to the fact that advance ticket sales reached a new Broadway record. But there was trouble on the road in Boston, none of it involving Julie. Burton was sure of his acting but not of his singing. Robert Goulet, making his Broadway début, *could* sing very well, but no one was too sure of his acting. Moss Hart had a heart attack and Alan Jay Lerner filled in as director.

Most of the problems were resolved, and the retitled show opened at the Majestic Theatre on 3 December 1960. Most critics agreed with Howard Taubman of the *New York Times*,

As Guinevere, with Robert Goulet (above) as Lancelot and Richard Burton (right) as King Arthur in *Camelot* 1961 UNITED PRESS INTERNATIONAL

who found *Camelot* only 'partly enchanted'. Of Lerner and Loewe, Taubman said, 'It would be unjust to tax them with not attaining the heights of *My Fair Lady*, but it cannot be denied that they miss their late collaborator, George Bernard Shaw.' Of Guinevere, he said, 'In the slim, airy person of Julie Andrews, a lovely actress and a true singer, she is regal and girlish, cool and eager.'

On the strength of its advance bookings and the drawing power of its stars (Goulet was hailed as the most exciting male newcomer in years, and Burton replaced Rex Harrison as the king of talk-singing), *Camelot* had a respectable two-year run. John F. Kennedy's love of the show and its original cast recording made *Camelot* legendary after his death, and his entire presidency was frequently referred to as 'Camelot'. It had many truly lovely songs that made it a better record than a show: 'I Loved You Once In Silence', 'If Ever I Would Leave You', 'Follow Me' and 'Before I Gaze At You Again'.

For Julie, a newly-wed ensconced with her Tony and a grey French poodle named Shy on a seventeenth-storey East Side apartment overlooking Welfare Island, 'it was a very pleasant time. *Camelot* was just about my size and weight, a good level for me, and I enjoyed it so much more than *My Fair Lady*.' Her eighteen-month run in her third hit musical in a row established Julie Andrews as the female musical comedy star of the period. She found 'working with Richard Burton was exciting,' and he termed her one of his 'three favourite co-stars, the others being P. O'Toole and E. Taylor.'

Burton also said that Julie Andrews was his only leading lady he'd never slept with. 'How dare he say such an awful thing about me?' was her retort.

During the creation of *Camelot* Julie established an important new friendship with T. H. 'Tim' White. He introduced her to the peacefulness of Alderney, and she bought a house there named Patmos. In 1962, towards the end of her run in *Camelot,* White pronounced her 'the most enchanting creature I have ever seen on stage'. He started to write a parody of

Cavalier poet Robert Herrick's 'Upon Julia's Clothes', the first line of which read: 'As in silks my Julia goes.' The second line of White's version was to have been an unflattering comment on Julie's nose, but he never finished it.

He did, however, write a poem entitled simply 'Julie Andrews', which appeared in a red-bound, privately printed volume of T. H. White's verse. She had number twenty-two of one hundred copies. A companion poem, dedicated to Richard Burton, appeared on the page facing White's tribute to her.

Julie Andrews

Helen, whose face was fatal, must have wept
Many long nights alone
And every night men died, she cried
And happy Paris kept sweet Helen.

Julie, the thousand prows aimed at her heart,
The tragic queen, comedian and clown,
Keeps Troy together, not apart
Nor lets one tower fall down.

5

JULIE AND CAROL AND MARY POPPINS

Julie made a guest appearance on Garry Moore's CBS television variety show in the spring of 1961, and she was such a success that Moore signed her for five additional visits the following season. In the first show's finale number, Julie teamed with Carol Burnett to sing 'Big D', the song about Dallas from Broadway's *Most Happy Fella*. The number, arranged by Ernie Flatt in unforgettable fashion, inspired the new duet to attempt a TV special of their own.

'Everybody was excited about it,' Carol Burnett recalled, 'except the networks. At the time, although I was a regular on the Garry Moore show, I wasn't yet under contract to CBS, and nobody had heard of Julie west of New Jersey. We went everywhere trying to sell the idea – to NBC, ABC and XYZ, but nobody was interested.' Mike Nichols, then half of a cabaret comedy team, had agreed to write the show, but even that potential contribution by Elaine May's partner moved no one to action.

In 1961 only NBC had regular network colour broadcasts,

and Burnett used that fact to tweak the CBS top management into a commitment. At a CBS network luncheon at the Waldorf-Astoria in New York, just after Christmas, Carol found herself the only woman at a table with James Aubrey, then president of CBS TV, Mike Dann, East Coast programming vice-president, and Oscar Katz, overall vice-president for network programmes.

'I was putting the three of them on, and they didn't realize it for a long time,' she remembered. 'I kept saying "It's a shame you boys passed up your chance at Julie and me, but then we do look so much better in colour anyway." They of course wanted to know what the hell I was talking about, and I told them that Julie and I were going to do a special. Aubrey asked why, and I said, "Because Julie and I have these magical powers." By then they had figured out that I might be putting them on.'

After lunch the three executives and Burnett found they had to walk back to CBS. 'Everyone was returning Christmas presents and you couldn't get a cab,' Carol recalled. 'When we got to the CBS building the men said, "We'll wait and get you a cab." I said, "Oh, don't worry, with my magical powers I'll probably get a ride." At that instant a beer truck appeared, and a big beefy driver with a tattoo yelled out, "Hey, Carol, you want a lift?" The men helped me into the cab of the beer truck, and I rode off to Central Park West, waving to the three of them standing there with their mouths open.'

The telephone in Carol's apartment rang less than an hour later. It was Katz, who said, 'You're a witch – you've got your special.'

'I called Julie at her dressing room at *Camelot* – it was a Wednesday, a matinée day – and there we were,' said Carol.

Julie and Carol at Carnegie Hall was a taped hour of songs and sketches from the stage of the famed New York concert hall, before a live invited audience. It was aired on the evening of 11 June 1962, near the close of Julie's *Camelot* run.

Sending up *The Sound of Music* in *Julie and Carol at Carnegie Hall*
1962 CBS TELEVISION

From the opening number, 'You're So London', chronicling
the opposite characteristics of the American Burnett and the
English Andrews ('You're so "hi, there, how are ya"/I'm so
"how t'y'do"; You're so Kensington Gardens and I'm so
San Antone' etc.) to the reprise of 'Big D', it was one of those
rare exhibitions of pure talent in total top form.

In 'The Nausiev Ballet', a Mike Nichols and Ken Welch
satire of touring Russian dance troupes, Julie proved the
equal of Carol in clowning, which wouldn't have surprised
English audiences but was a first in America for her. Julie did
just one solo, an exquisite 'Johnny's So Long at the Fair'. She
and Carol did a devastating parody of *The Sound of Music,*
then the biggest hit on Broadway (eclipsing both *Camelot* and
something like the seventh company of *My Fair Lady*). In
'The Pratt Family of Switzerland', Julie played the Maria Von
Trapp prototype in her best Mary Martin manner, and Carol

played Cynthia, the only girl among seventeen Pratt boys. The Nichols–Welch songs were perfect send-ups of the Rodgers and Hammerstein score that in three years Julie would have to sing straight.

The Carnegie Hall programme showed American audiences a new Andrews versatility, and it was a total critical triumph for both stars. The show won an Emmy Award, and gave Mike Nichols a big push in his desired transition from performer to writer-director. Both Burnett and Nichols became close friends of Julie and Tony. The material held up so well on the Columbia cast recording that *Julie and Carol at Carnegie Hall* became television's only classic sound-track and was still selling, and featured in the record company catalogue, twenty years later.

Even in these early years of their marriage, Julie made considerably more money than Tony, but said 'this has never made any difference. I get mine in chunks; he gets his regularly, and I expect he'll work far longer than I will.' The two salaries were kept separate and, by mutual agreement, money was seldom discussed by the Waltons. 'If Tony minds my being Julie Andrews he certainly doesn't let me know it,' she said in 1961.

Tony was beginning to make a reputation as a set and costume designer in the theatre, with shows such as *Valmouth* in London, and *Golden Boy* on Broadway. And her marriage, Julie said, 'helped me stand on my own two feet'. She became pregnant early in 1962, and soon motherhood would add a new dimension to her life, without really interrupting the fast climb of her career.

Walt Disney went to see a Wednesday matinée of *Camelot* that spring of 1962. Disney, who never worried about having stars in his movies because his own name as producer guaranteed success at the box office, was looking for an actress to play Mary Poppins. Like all Disney movies involving animation, *Mary Poppins* had been brewing for some time until all the elements were just right. Watching Julie in the theatre –

Carol and Julie in the finale at Carnegie Hall
1962 CBS TELEVISION

particularly during the 'What Do the Simple Folk Do?' number – convinced Disney that he had found his Mary. He felt that she had the right kind of sense of humour, and was impressed with her whistling ability in that sprightly number, whistling being very helpful to nannies. Disney visited Julie's dressing room after the show, discussed the Poppins role briefly, and invited her and Tony to visit him at the Disney studios in Burbank.

'Since I had never made a movie the idea appealed to me greatly,' she said. 'I had thought a lot about movies, but never very seriously. I had *fantasies* that I'd make a movie someday, but I had no serious intentions of making them.'

'She was always putting herself down about movies,' Carol Burnett remembered, 'never thinking she would look good enough. When the Poppins part came up she asked me, "Do you think I ought to? Go to work for Walt Disney? The cartoon person?" I assured her that Disney did other things besides cartoons, but she was a little worried about it. But when she came out to Hollywood she became totally enthusiastic. I don't think she ever came out here to be the great big star of the world, but she was very excited about that one movie.'

'I must say I will be forever grateful to that man,' Julie said of Disney. 'Tony and I flew out after *Camelot* to take a look, and liked it enormously. It was so easy to see what he was trying to do with *Mary Poppins*, and I loved that very slight flavour of vaudeville to it.'

Tony was offered a job as overall design director, so that the couple could be together with their new-born child, who was due in November. They were entertained lavishly at Disney's watchful insistence. But it was the Robert and Richard Sherman music that really convinced Julie. 'I was sold,' she said. She signed a contract for $150,000 for the film, plus a living allowance, since she was technically a resident of London temporarily stationed in New York. Tony got a separate fee for his set and costume design work. Then the couple

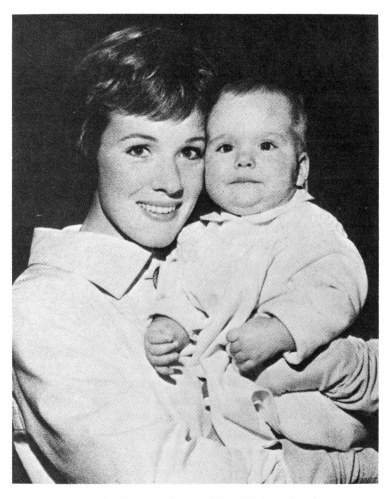

With one-year-old daughter Emma Kate Walton, leaving
New York on the way to Hollywood and *Mary Poppins*
1963 UNITED PRESS INTERNATIONAL

returned to London, to have their first baby.

Emma Kate came on 27 November 1962, at the London
Clinic. Julie had mothered her three younger brothers, particularly Chris, who was eleven years younger than she, and
she attributed her notable whistling ability to those three

boys. She had long wanted children of her own, and she wanted more than one. 'I'd like a family of three or five boys,' she said, 'weather and tide permitting, as we say in England. Tony wants girls. I just want a family of little Tonys.'

Pamela Travers, then fifty-nine years old, was the author of the Mary Poppins books on which the Disney movie was to be based. Legally she had nothing to say about who played the leading role. Nevertheless, 'she rang me up in the hospital the day after I had Emma,' Julie recalled. 'She said, "P. Travers here. Speak to me. I want to hear your voice." I was still too weak from giving birth and I told her I wanted to recover first. When we finally got together the first thing she said was, "Well, you've got the nose for it." I adored her. She was so honest and direct. Tony and I had several lunches with her before we went to Hollywood to do the movie. Later I wrote her a long letter from the set and tried to give her a sort of idea of what we were doing.'

The family of three, Tony, Julie and Emma Kate, settled into a rented house in Studio City, in the San Fernando Valley of Los Angeles, with a nanny and a maid, in mid 1963. They had six months of rest in Alderney behind them. It was pleasant for both parents, working at the Disney Studios in Burbank, even though *My Fair Lady* was in pre-production, with a new Eliza, at Warner Brothers, less than a mile away.

'It may have been that celebrated ill wind,' Julie said, years later. 'I had *Mary Poppins* to soften the blow.'

My Fair Lady was the one movie she had hoped for, and not being familiar with the motion picture business, even in Britain, Julie didn't really understand the Hollywood star system that had worked against her. Warner Brothers had invested a record $5,500,000 in acquiring the screen rights to the musical. And Jack Warner, head of the studio and the producer of *My Fair Lady* as well, was determined to use Rex Harrison as Henry Higgins. Harrison was not a potent box office name in America, but no one else could come close to playing the part, Warner felt. But a string of fair ladies had followed Julie on

Mary Poppins 1964 WALT DISNEY PRODUCTIONS

Broadway, and done Eliza rather well. So the feeling at Warner Brothers was that, while it might have been difficult to 'get' the role on stage, any number of stars who were also good actresses could probably get by on screen, especially under George Cukor's direction.

Julie stayed in the running for the $17 million production (then a record for a movie), simply because she had been brilliant in the part for three and a half years. That just made it harder to take when Audrey Hepburn got the part – and a fee of $1 million. Hepburn was not even going to do all her own singing; that job would fall once again to Marni Nixon, the mimic ghost-singer in a slew of movie musicals – without formal acknowledgement or screen credit, as usual.

The morning she found out about Audrey's casting, Julie was in her agent's office for a conference. He and his associates already knew about the announcement and assumed Julie did. But she didn't, and asked how *My Fair Lady* was going.

'Haven't you heard?' someone said. 'They've signed Audrey Hepburn'.

'Oh, . . . I see,' was the quiet, composed reply, as Julie struggled to get hold of herself. After a pause, she said, 'Well, that's that, isn't it?'

Later that same morning, Julie was riding by the Warner Brothers studios. Out of a protracted, deliberate silence came, in a crystalline, high-pitched voice, 'And a good morning to you, Mr Warner, and the best of luck.'

Julie often said that if it had been anyone but Audrey Hepburn, an actress she didn't know but did admire, she 'would have been blazing mad. Of course I wanted to play it. Who wouldn't want to play Eliza? But in a way it's a good thing having to play a different role. People at least will know I can do something else.'

Logistically, it would have been possible for Julie to have played both Eliza and Mary Poppins, because principal photography involving Eliza didn't begin until Julie's part in

With Dick Van Dyke, Karen Dotrice and Matthew Garber in *Mary Poppins*
1964 WALT DISNEY PRODUCTIONS

Mary Poppins was completed. However, she could not have played Eliza and done either *The Americanization of Emily* or *The Sound of Music*. 'I was more than compensated by three marvellous roles,' she said. During the making of *Mary Poppins* she had been 'surprised by the amount of interest in me from the other studios'. Disney had been showing rough cuts and rushes to other producers, a highly unusual practice, and as a result of these informal previews Julie had been signed for both *Emily* and *The Sound of Music* long before *Mary Poppins* had been released.

In the original Mary Poppins book published in 1934, P. L. ('Don't call me Miss or Mrs, just P.L.') Travers had described Mary as having 'shiny black hair, like a wooden Dutch doll, with large hands and feet, pink cheeks and round blue eyes. She is a plain 27-year-old who obviously has assumed all the prerogatives of a pretty woman, because everybody falls in love with her.' Except for the black hair, Julie proved to be close casting; she was even 27 when she began shooting the film. Julie said that her characterization of the acid-tongued no-nonsense nanny was 'a little softer, a little rounder' than in the books.

Disney made other changes from the Travers originals: the setting was taken from the 1930s back to Edwardian London because it was more photogenic and minus the Depression; the Banks family house where the nanny works went from 'rather dilapidated' and needing a coat of paint to a sumptuous, velvet-lined Edwardian mansion. But the friendship between Mary Poppins and Bert, the chimney sweep (Dick Van Dyke) remained platonic, to P.L.'s great relief.

The number of children in the household was reduced from four to two (Matthew Garber and Karen Dotrice); their parents (Glynis Johns and David Tomlinson) were turned into a neglectful suffragette and businessman respectively. The writers took these dramatic liberties, they said, to introduce a bit of 'harmless' conflict, and to allow Mary to arrive, wind-borne by an umbrella, to save her charges from this

Mary Poppins with her two charges among the rooftops of London
1964 WALT DISNEY PRODUCTIONS

Mary Poppins 1964 WALT DISNEY PRODUCTIONS

neglect. As in the book, however, nearly everyone floated in the air at some time or other (most memorably during Ed Wynn's tea-party on the ceiling), and Mary Poppins could do it at will.

'At first I missed the live audience reaction,' said Julie of her first movie experience. 'But as I grew accustomed to the medium, I found myself enjoying movie-making more and more. One thing that appealed to me particularly was the permanence. If your performance was good, it was preserved for posterity. Another wonderful thing about movies is that you don't have to be in perfect voice every night.'

Although Tony was costume designer on Mary Poppins, he and Julie rarely saw each other during working hours. Most of his work was, of course, done before the actual shooting began. Since they were brand-new parents, both working in movies for the first time, the situation put an obvious strain on the marriage. Though they seldom talked about it, they both knew well the underlying fact that Tony would never have been hired as scenic designer for the picture had his wife not been playing the leading role.

During filming Julie took great delight in shrieking the highest note she could reach, like a factory whistle, into the microphone hanging over her head. All her co-workers were amused – bar one: the sound technician with his earphones on. 'Usually, he'd have to go away for almost half an hour to recover,' she said.

It didn't take the shrewd businessmen at Walt Disney studios even that long to realize what they had on their hands with *Mary Poppins*. In the summer of 1964, preparing for a late-September release, they set an exploitation budget that was 'more than for any other picture' released by the company. They signed contracts for thirty-eight separate Mary Poppins products, including girls' dresses, dolls, houseware, jewellry and four million books reprinted by various publishers.

The picture opened at Radio City Music Hall in New York,

and then around the United States, to almost unanimously glowing reviews. A few critics took issue with the interpretation of the Poppins stories, but Bosley Crowther of the *New York Times* was not among them. He said:

'In case you are a Mary Poppins zealot who dotes on her just as she is, don't let the intrusion of Mr Disney and his myrmidons worry you one bit. Be thankful for it and praise heaven that they are still making films. For the visual and aural felicities they have added to this sparkling colour film – the enchantments of beautiful production, some deliciously animated sequences, some exciting and nimble dancing and a spinning musical score – make it the nicest entertainment that has opened at the Music Hall this year. . . .

'This is the genuine Mary Poppins that comes sailing in on an east wind . . . played superbly by Miss Andrews, with her button-shoed feet splayed out to give her an unshakeable footing and a look of complete authority, who calmly proceeds to show her charges that wonders will never cease and that there's nothing like a spoonful of sugar to sweeten the medicine.'

My Fair Lady opened in mid October 1964, just a month after *Mary Poppins*, and to even more lavish praise. Audrey Hepburn's acting and Marni Nixon's singing got good notices, perhaps not so much because they were good as that they weren't as bad as Andrews partisans had feared. Julie went to see *My Fair Lady* and pronounced it 'a wonderful film. It was the first time I had ever seen it from the front. Now I know why people are so crazy about it.' Of the dubbed singing, she said neutrally, 'I think dubbing is fine as long as you can get away with it.'

Audrey Hepburn returned the compliment, by slipping into Radio City Music Hall unnoticed, with her then husband Mel Ferrer, while *Mary Poppins* was playing. 'We were in such a hurry that we could only stay an hour,' Hepburn recounted, 'but Julie was simply wonderful, and Mel thought so too.'

So much for the feud between Julie and Audrey that many members of the press, particularly in Europe, had tried to stir up. But Hollywood was still going to have its revenge on Jack Warner, and, indirectly, on Audrey Hepburn. When the Academy Award nominations for 1964 were announced in February of 1965, *My Fair Lady* was nominated in every major category *except* Best Actress, and Julie Andrews was nominated for Best Actress in *Mary Poppins*. With Audrey Hepburn not in the running, Julie was the heavy favourite to win from the moment nominations were out.

Tony Walton was nominated for Best Costume Design for *Mary Poppins*, which itself was nominated for Best Picture of 1964, along with *Dr Strangelove, Becket, Zorba the Greek* and *My Fair Lady*.

At the Hollywood Foreign Press Association Golden Globes Awards, which were held between the Oscar nominations and the Awards themselves, Julie won the award for Best Actress in a Musical. She thanked, among others, 'Jack Warner, for making it all possible'. Warner, who received the Best Musical award for *My Fair Lady* 'was sitting right in front of me – it was grand fun,' Julie said. Her press agents swore that the whole idea of the acceptance had been hers, and she never denied it.

The high preponderance of overseas, particularly British, nominees prompted Master of Ceremonies Bob Hope to quip, on Academy Awards night (5 April 1965): 'Tonight Hollywood is handing out foreign aid.' And for the next three hours it did just that.

Tony Walton lost to a fellow Briton, Cecil Beaton, who had designed the costumes for both stage and screen versions of *My Fair Lady*. 'Oh, no, Tony,' Julie said softly to her husband when Beaton's name was announced. Tony applauded dutifully.

'Chim Chim Cheree' from *Mary Poppins* won the Best Song Oscar for the Shermans, but otherwise it was mostly *My Fair Lady*'s night. George Cukor won his first Oscar for

Julie Andrews and Jack Warner congratulate each other on their Oscars (Best Actress in a Musical for Mary Poppins, and Best Musical for *My Fair Lady*) 1965 WIDE WORLD PHOTOS

directing, and Audrey Hepburn (a previous winner, in 1953 for *Roman Holiday*) got to present the Best Actor Oscar to Rex Harrison. A beaming Harrison bounded onto the stage to be hugged and kissed by his unnominated but clearly delighted co-star. 'I have to thank two fair ladies, I think,' said Harrison. 'Oh, yes,' said Hepburn.

Warner's acceptance of the Best Picture Oscar for *My Fair Lady* proved to be an anti-climax. His speech made no reference to his cast, and was delivered in the self-confident tones of a successful businessman being congratulated on a worth-while $17-million investment. He paid tribute to 'the many people who contributed to *My Fair Lady*', without naming names.

The highlight of the evening was the virtual crowning of a new queen of movieland. When Harrison's name had been announced the ABC TV cameras had caught Julie in close-up, licking a very dry, very stiff upper lip. When her own name was announced as Best Actress for her first motion picture, she was suddenly all smiles: the earlier nervousness was gone. *En route* to posing for pictures with Harrison, with their gold Oscar statuettes (as she surely would have done had she played Eliza again), Julie thanked her audience for the warmest possible welcome to Hollywood: 'You Americans are famous for your hospitality,' she said, 'but this is ridiculous.'

6

EMILY AND THE SOUND OF MONEY

'SCARED to death' at first, Julie went straight from *Mary Poppins* into *The Americanization of Emily*, the story of a young English Second World War widow who worked as a motor-pool driver for American Navy officers in England during the day, and who sometimes, out of kindness, slept with them at night – especially if she thought they were doomed to be killed in battle. Paddy Chayefsky had written the screenplay from a novel by William Bradford Huie, embellishing it in the process with an anti-war message of his own.

'I was at a loss without songs,' said Julie. 'At least in *Mary Poppins* I would always take comfort in the knowledge that I would be doing a song and would feel secure eventually, but in *Emily* there were no songs to hang on to.'

Marty Ransohoff, the most independent of independent producers, had made a fortune on several hit television series and made money on his first six pictures. He rented his offices at, and released most of his pictures through, Metro-Goldwyn-Mayer, and his associate John Calley called Ransohoff, who had previously been a small-time businessman in Connecticut, 'an L. B. Mayer without overheads'.

'He speaks for himself,' said Julie, 'he stands or falls by himself. He didn't depend on anybody to achieve his success. And if you don't like it, he couldn't care less.' Ransohoff took chances with his movies – *The Loved One* and *Catch-22* among them – 'and he certainly took a chance on me. A lot of people told Marty he was out of his mind to pick me. When I read the script I got very excited about it, but I didn't think I had much chance to get the part.'

One of those who thought she was wrong for it was Blake Edwards, a writer-director she had met only once at that point. Edwards was asked his opinion on Julie for the Emily role and said, 'No, I don't think she's right.' Years later he said, 'And she wasn't right in terms of the screenplay. I would have bet you against her doing it well, which is interesting now. But she brought something to it that changed Emily without changing the screenplay, and it worked.'

But Ransohoff, like Robert Wise and others, had seen forty minutes of rough-cut footage of *Mary Poppins*. 'After three minutes of the stuff I knew Julie was our girl,' he said. 'I just took that one look and knew she was right for Emily. She did not generate obvious, overt sexuality. She is not a sex symbol, but she has a classic sensuousness. She also had a certain refinement – another classic quality – rather than an over-abundance of physical equipment, which gave her a great deal of sex appeal, slightly more refined and highbred than most.'

James Garner, the nominal star of the film, had co-star approval written into his contract, and could have vetoed the movie unknown. He didn't, because he was playing in *The Caine Mutiny Court Martial* on Broadway at the same time as Julie was appearing, just up the street, in *My Fair Lady*. 'I didn't know her, but I had seen her in it,' Garner recalled, 'and that was good enough for me.'

Garner was another gamble for Ransohoff; a successful television star who had done mostly comedy roles in movies,

The Americanization of Emily 1964 METRO-GOLDWYN-MAYER

Garner was not the obvious choice for a serious dramatic film. In *Emily* he played Lieutenant Commander Charlie Madison, nominally an aide to a Navy Rear-Admiral (Melvyn Douglas), but actually a 'dog robber', a procurer of everything from perfume to the people who wear it. Madison was also an advocate of open cowardice, a doctrine of self-preservation that was counter to the prevailing wartime philosophy, especially in England. As Charlie, James Garner gave the best performance of his career.

In a scene set in Madison's hotel room (which looked more like a black-market clearing house), Chayefsky's script satirized both the British and Americans, a sequence that Andrews and Garner handled particularly well. Emily made caustic comments about the avariciousness and rule-bending of Americans, and Madison took down the English for their anti-American ingratitude, unconcealed jealousy and self-imposed stiff-upper-lip martyrdom. At the same time they began to fall in love.

It was important to Ransohoff to film this movie in black and white, at a time when every kind of movie, even the cheapest B cops-and-robbers story, was being filmed in colour, with an eye to television sales. It turned out to be the only film that Julie Andrews made that wasn't in colour.

During shooting she still worried about 'the absence of an audience. The audience gives you a push; it makes you realize you've got to do it right – there will be no second time. Still, I love the feeling in movies of doing something fresh every day, instead of the same thing. I find movie work much more exhausting than I had expected. I suppose my own nervous tension has a good deal to do with it. And the only way I can ease the tension is to sing, hum or whistle. I wonder sometimes what will happen when I do something in the theatre again. Will I feel nervous in front of an audience?'

Julie's tension-breaking singing and whistling (and sometimes just a high note held as long as possible) were done right on the set, in full hearing of cast and crew. One day as a

With James Garner in *The Americanization of Emily*
1964 METRO-GOLDWYN-MAYER

With James Garner and Joyce Grenfell in
The Americanization of Emily
1964 CULVER PICTURES

camera was being reloaded Julie broke into a faultless chorus
of 'Melancholy Baby'. Garner and director Arthur Hiller
were delighted to suspend work in favour of a free Julie
Andrews concert, but she was totally oblivious to their watching her take this unusual tranquilliser for her taut nerves.

Julie did remember being unhappy about one scene that
was already 'in the can'. 'Marty and I were watching the
rushes together, and I was not happy about it at all. We had
them set up the scene again the next day so I could do it all

With producer Marty Ransohoff on the set of *The Americanization of Emily*
1964 METRO-GOLDWYN-MAYER

over again. I'm not at all sure that it was any better the second time, but it was my whim and he indulged it.'

'Arthur Hiller and I thought the scene had worked well,' Ransohoff recalled, 'but Julie thought it could be done another way. So I gave her and the crew a day to restage and reshoot the scene her way. When we saw the rough cut of the whole movie a few weeks later, her scene wasn't in it. I had used the original scene. She burst out laughing. She just couldn't understand why I would re-do the scene and spend all that money if I was so sure I was right. I told her that it was just that the values in the original were the ones we wanted. Instead of having a big ego attitude, she just laughed. She completely respected my position, but the shock of realizing "Oh, my God, we've thrown a whole day away" sent her into hysterics.'

James Garner, who waited eighteen years to work with her again in *Victor, Victoria*, recalled 'the first love scene she'd ever done in a movie, and her first real love scene anywhere. She knows only one way to do something – and that's right. In reality she's not like what she's like on screen – certainly not in *Mary Poppins* – but nobody does it better than Julie can. Julie's a little bit more natural at anything than anybody else.'

Even before *Emily* was released, Marty Ransohoff was convinced that Julie Andrews would be the next movie superstar. 'She's the most exciting thing I've seen in ten years. There's an open honesty in her face that's like magic – it lights up the screen.' He also found her easy to work with, 'a dream. She is co-operative and has ideas, and is anxious to help. All conversations with her are on an intellectual level. She brings quality to a project. She's infectious around the set, with a sense of humour that has a great effect on other performers and a great positiveness both behind the scenes and in front of the camera. A film can be damaged by a growler, but Julie lifts up a production. She is totally lacking in the kind of ego that says she knows it all and is always right.'

Garner agreed. 'An actor working opposite Julie might

The Americanization of Emily 1964 METRO-GOLDWYN-MAYER

worry about being acted into the draperies. I didn't and wouldn't compete with Julie on those terms for two reasons – I might lose, and I wouldn't care. Julie is a very strong-willed girl, but she manages her life so you are never offended by her strong will.'

The Americanization of Emily opened in the winter of 1964–5, smack between *Mary Poppins* and *The Sound of Music*. It was overshadowed by both and the reviews were decidedly mixed. Some critics were confused by the intent of the screenplay, the apparent seriousness of the anti-war theme, and what they considered a sell-out ending. Some saw the Andrews performance as bland and stereotyped, but most agreed that in terms of her comic and dramatic ability she could have a career in movies, even if she never sang again.

'It wasn't that I was so good,' Julie said, 'it was just such a surprise to see me in it. I don't think of myself as any great shakes as an actress. That's why I consider myself lucky when an *Emily* comes along. I'd love to do more serious roles like that. But films like *Emily* aren't available too readily. The script was so good; it had something to say.'

'I wasn't trying to say a damned thing in *The Sound of Music*,' director Robert Wise said. 'That's as good a face as I can put on it. People just feel good when they see it; there's a sense of warmth, of well-being, of happiness and joy.'

Julie did not greet the prospect of playing Maria in *The Sound of Music* with great joy, although her competitive spirit was at work in the effort. At a luncheon Darryl Zanuck and several other Twentieth Century-Fox executives held to discuss the part, Wise pointedly announced that the film versions of *The Sound of Music* and *My Fair Lady* would be showing in New York at the same time on opposite sides of Broadway – and then sat back and awaited the reaction. 'Julie looked at each of us in turn without speaking,' he recalled. 'Then she threw back her head and laughed. "All right then. Let's show them, eh, fellows?" That was the new Julie Andrews talking.'

The title-song sequence in *The Sound of Music*
1965 TWENTIETH CENTURY-FOX

'We were always putting *The Sound of Music* down,' said Carol Burnett, 'and Julie always made fun of that happy nun. I'm not sure Richard Rodgers was awfully pleased when she was offered the movie. And I think he was concerned about her being Gwendolyn Goodie Two-Shoes. She sent me pictures from Austria of her in her nun's habit, which was a big laugh.'

'I thought it might be awfully saccharine,' Julie said, 'After all, what can you do with nuns, seven children and Austria? But Bob Wise decided to get rid of the sugar – no filigree, no carved wood, no Swiss chalets, and he stuck to his guns. We all felt the same way. It helped that it was a motion picture because they could do such sweeping things visually.'

Wise cast Julie (Broadway's original Maria, Mary Martin, was then fifty years old and not considered for the movie) on the basis of the Disney footage. He also insisted on Christopher Plummer, a distinguished Canadian actor not known for musicals and hardly a major movie marquee name, for the role of Captain Georg von Trapp. 'I wanted the character to have bite, incisiveness and real dimension,' he said. 'I felt we must go on the basis of the story, and not bastardize it with just big names.'

Julie was paid a relatively modest $225,000, a flat fee with no participation in the movie's profits, and the other actors (who included Peggy Wood as the Mother Abbess, Eleanor Parker as the Baroness that von Trapp doesn't marry, and Richard Haydn as the impresario who helps the family escape to Switzerland) were paid accordingly. Wise was working towards 10 per cent of the net profits; his share would be more than $10 million. And the four producers of the Broadway version of *The Sound of Music* – including Richard Rodgers, the estate of Oscar Hammerstein, and Richard Halliday, Mary Martin's husband – collectively received 10 per cent of the gross.

Filming started in the spring of 1964, and eleven weeks of the twenty-two week shooting schedule were spent on loca-

Singing the 'Do, Re, Mi' number in *The Sound of Music*
1965 TWENTIETH CENTURY-FOX

tion in Salzburg, Austria. Julie, despite her earlier reservations had a 'larky time'. Wise remembered that she 'always enjoyed a good laugh with the kids. She had marvellous fun in her, and in addition to humour, she had warmth and understanding.'

The first sequence shot was of Julie and the seven von Trapp children bundled up in Maria's bed during a bad thunderstorm, with her singing 'My Favourite Things'. 'I was having trouble getting the proper reactions from two of the kids,' Wise said. 'All of a sudden I heard this shrill laugh in back of me. It was Julie, putting on an act to make the kids laugh. She did it without announcing it to me or anyone else, but she put the kids at ease and made them easier to work with.'

In her own attempt to de-sweeten *The Sound of Music* Julie focused on the 'My Favourite Things' sequence. 'Maria *couldn't* be sweetness and light with seven kids on her hands all the time. Seven kids would have to get on one's nerves, so I tried once in a while to show that I might be slightly exhausted ,by them. On the bed, when they ask me to do this or that and say "What kind of things do you mean?", just before I go into "My Favourite Things", I thought, "Oh my God! Children always do ask questions like that. Maria must have had moments when she bordered on being tired and cross."'

The film gave Julie a chance to cut her hair very short, 'something I'd always wanted to do, though having to bleach it blond was a bit of a shocker, especially my first sight of it.'

She also experimented with variations on vaudeville bits from her girlhood, like catching her guitar case crosswise in the door of the bus Maria takes from the Abbey to the von Trapp house. Wise disqualified that Buster Keatonism in what was supposed to be a solemn moment, but allowed another: when Maria turns away from the Mother Superior, who has told her she must be a governess, the gangly novitiate sees a post just in time to sidestep it – thereby giving the character a tiny added dimension of confusion.

With Christopher Plummer and the rest of the von Trapp family in *The Sound of Music* 1965 TWENTIETH CENTURY-FOX

'She must have 8,000 bits,' said one crew member. Many of them took place off camera. One day, to clear tension before a complicated camera move, she did a deliberate trip and fell flat on her face. She was versatile enough, on another occasion, to pratfall on the other side. To portray Maria, Julie had learned a bit of guitar, and one day she flung it aside to fly into an impromptu flamenco dance – still wearing her postulant's habit and high button shoes.

Scheduled to drive to Munich one weekend to see her friend Svetlana Beriosova dance with the Royal Ballet on tour, Julie instead hired a bus, and took thirty chums from the cast and crew. Throughout the sixty-mile trip from Salzburg to Munich she imitated an English sightseeing coach conductor, sometimes lapsing into bits of cockney. On the return trip to Salzburg, Julie led group singing and soloed on some cockney songs.

'It rained nearly every day we were in Austria,' Julie recalled, 'and did terrible things to our nerves.' The rain was at its worst during the shooting of the unforgettable opening sequence of *The Sound of Music*, where the helicopter containing the camera swoops down over the Alps to catch Maria dancing bareheaded in forbidden fields while she sings the title song. There were several days when Julie and the crew would have to wait out the rain before she could go tripping over the mountains again.

On these occasions Julie, associate producer (and musical director) Saul Chaplin, and co-choreographer Marc Breaux, would sing songs on the rainy hillside for hours. She considered the trio's harmonies so good, particularly on the 'Hawaiian War Chant', that she named the group the Vocalzones. She also did solos, such as 'The Bell Song' from *Lakme*, in pure operatic style, exquisitely on every note, but with the mannerisms and facial expressions of a twelve-year-old child surprised at the power of her own voice. And she sang the 'Indian Love Call' slightly off-key.

'These things were all spontaneous, and they related to the situation at the moment,' Julie said. 'If the situation is getting depressing, or people are getting pesky or touchy, a little fun always helps. I'll do anything I can think of to relieve any kind of tension.'

Dorothy Jeakins, the costume designer on the picture, and later on *Hawaii*, led the cheering section of Julie's admirers. 'She's extremely pure, extremely human,' said Jeakins. 'Julie has great zeal and spirit. She's ethereal, yet down to earth. Everything she does is fresh and impromptu – and gone – like a whistle or a laugh.'

The Sound of Music 1965 TWENTIETH CENTURY-FOX

Some on the set of *The Sound of Music* found Julie's chumminess compulsive ('I've never worked with anyone who said "thank you" so much,' said one veteran grip), and others didn't believe it. 'She may be a nun,' said one, 'but she's a nun with a switchblade.'

Christopher Plummer called her 'terribly nice, but terribly nervous', and told his wife that working with her was 'like being hit over the head every day with a Hallmark card'.

Plummer was having problems on the picture, primarily because he had expected to do his own singing on 'The Sound of Music' and 'Edelweiss', each of which he was to sing twice in the film. Plummer's songs were dubbed in by a singer of commercials, and the actor, according to a friend, 'was so fed up he began calling it *The Sound of Mucus*'.

'Julie knew how a character should be played,' said Wise, 'and she would fight to have it played right. We thrashed it out; she gave some and I gave some.' Wise was frankly surprised by 'the range of her talent, the depth of it, especially in emotional scenes', and called her 'the most unaffected player I'd ever worked with. She was so down to earth, pleasant and natural, it was hard to believe she was really Julie Andrews. She had an open, warm response to work, but then she was used to working, to getting on with the job.'

Richard Rodgers had written both the words and music for two new songs in the movie version of *The Sound of Music*. (Four of the stage version's songs had been dropped.) Both songs, 'I Have Confidence' and 'Something Good', were for Julie, and she liked them both. Her singing of each, the former with sunny bravado, the latter with quiet gratitude, summarized both her approach and appropriateness to the venture. Maria on screen was a part Julie Andrews was born to play.

Her success in it (for the next several years it was the most successful movie ever made, and she was the world's biggest star) was attributable, Wise thought, to a 'genuineness about her, an unphoniness. What you see on the screen is an exten-

With Christopher Plummer in *The Sound of Music*
1965 TWENTIETH CENTURY-FOX

sion of Julie herself. She goes right through the camera onto film and out to the audience. Julie seems to have been born with that magic gene that comes through on screen; this magic gene, whatever it is coming through, commands you to react abnormally to her.'

Tony Walton, who had moved back to New York after *Mary Poppins* despite another film offer from Julie's agent, escorted Julie to the New York première of *The Sound of Music* at the Rivoli Theatre, in March 1965. The première, for which Julie had flown in from California (with Emma Kate and her nanny), was a star-studded, klieg-lighted event in the old Hollywood style, full of the highest expectations. Those attending included Helen Hayes, Beatrice Lillie, Adlai Stevenson, Salvador Dali, Samuel Goldwyn, and, of course, Richard Rodgers. Bette Davis called Julie 'one of the loveliest things I've ever seen'. And Mrs Oscar Hammerstein spoke for the majority about the movie: 'I'll have to drag out all those old superlatives about Hollywood. It's as close to perfection as any movie musical I've ever seen. The beauty of it is that you really see Austria – the streams, the valleys and mountains are the real thing. I know Oscar would have loved it.'

Thus no one at the opening was prepared for what happened the next day, least of all Robert Wise and Darryl Zanuck. Every major national film critic in America hated *The Sound of Music*. Typical of the reaction was that of the New York *Herald Tribune*'s Judith Crist, who wrote: 'One star and much scenery do not a two-hour-and-fifty-minutes-plus-intermission entertainment make, and the issue must be faced. Squarely. That is the way to face *The Sound of Music*. This last, most remunerative and least inspired, let alone sophisticated, of the Rodgers and Hammerstein collaborations is square and solid sugar. Calorie-counters, diabetics and grown-ups from eight to eighty had best beware.'

In fact, nobody liked *The Sound of Music*, except the public. The critics had never been so powerless to influence

108

opinion concerning a movie. Advance ticket sales at the Rivoli, already substantial in anticipation of Easter, increased in geometric proportion to the negative notices. And the pattern was repeated throughout the world, where the picture showed at an astonishing 3,200 theatres, almost one-tenth of the total of 35,000. It broke box office records in twenty-nine countries, including Britain, where it doubled the gross of any other film in that country; and Thailand, where it was called *Charms of the Heaven-Sound* (at the Bangkok première King Bhumibol, whose predecessor was the subject of the best of all Rodgers and Hammerstein musicals, played 'Do, Re, Mi' on his clarinet).

Multiple visits to the film by individual fans helped boost the box office total of the picture, and it soon surpassed *Gone With the Wind* as the most popular movie of all time; it was surpassed itself only in the late 1970s and early 1980s by *Star Wars, The Empire Strikes Back, Jaws* and *Raiders of the Lost Ark* – it even lost the distinction of being the most popular movie musical to *Grease*. Many people saw *The Sound of Music* one hundred times or more, but the clear champion viewer was the woman in Wales who went at least once a day for more than a year. The sound-track record album became the best-selling album of all time, beating out the original Broadway cast of *My Fair Lady*. The record had sold fifteen million units by the time the movie played on network television in 1976; half a million were sold in the weeks immediately following the telecast.

It was hard to explain the phenomenal success of *The Sound of Music*, even for those involved. 'Who knows?' asked the director, to whom most of the credit was given. Wise won almost every award it is possible to win as producer or director, including the Directors' Guild of America Best Director Award for 1966, and two Oscars, one as director, and one for Best Picture.

The Academy Awards were highly responsive to the box office record of *The Sound of Music*, which had been out for

109

The Sound of Music 1965 TWENTIETH CENTURY-FOX

more than a year by Oscar time 1966. It received ten nominations (to eleven for *Doctor Zhivago*, another box office smash, but one that had achieved some praise from critics), including one for Julie as Best Actress. That gave her a shot to become the first actress to win back-to-back Oscars since Luise Rainer had done it in 1936 and 1937 with *The Great Zeigfeld* and *The Good Earth*.

Julie attended the Oscars, with Saul Chaplin, in a triple role: as presenter of the Best Actor award, as nominee, and as substitute acceptor for Robert Wise (who was on location with *The Sand Pebbles* in Hong Kong). Her chief competition was another English Julie – Christie for her work in *Darling*. Both Julies were highly conspicuous, Christie in a pair of gold lamé self-designed pyjamas that made her *look* like an Oscar, and Andrews in a Dorothy Jeakins designed reddish-orange lightweight wool dress with a discotheque back and a deep-V 'wrapped' front.

In her ninth row aisle seat at the ceremonies, Julie Andrews kept wringing her hands together, as Chaplin smiled and tried to soothe her nerves. When the editing award went to William Reynolds for *The Sound of Music,* Julie shouted, 'Oh boy,' and clapped so wildly that she knocked her white mink to the floor. Reynolds, in accepting the award, complimented her by saying, 'When in doubt, cut to Julie Andrews.' After accepting for Wise, she waited backstage for the Best Actress award, to be announced by Rex Harrison. 'Julie,' he said with lips pursed, then he paused for a perverse split second before adding '. . . Christie, for *Darling*.' Moments later, when *The Sound of Music* won the Oscar as Best Picture of 1965, for a total of five Academy Awards, Julie Andrews said 'Oh boy' again. 'We did it. Isn't that great? Now I'm happy.'

7

SVENGALI AND PSYCHOANALYSIS

WITH three successful movies behind her, three more lined up (the last putting her in the $1 million per picture category), more scripts than she could read, an Oscar, and unbridled acclaim from the press and public, Julie Andrews should have been sublimely happy. Seemingly effortlessly, she had become the superstar she had clearly set out to be. She bought a new house on a hillside in Coldwater Canyon, just north of Beverly Hills, and lived there with Emma Kate, a nanny and a butler. A secretary came in daily, and Julie had agents and a business manager who adored her and whom she trusted. Tony was still in New York, but in touch almost daily by taped letters or the telephone.

'I was desperately unhappy,' she recalled, 'and there was no apparent reason for it. I was successful and I should have been happy. I just felt this depression. I was behaving in a way that scared hell out of me. It's terrible when all those lovely things are happening to you and you aren't enjoying them. I didn't like myself very much, and I was probably getting too big for my boots. I felt I needed some serious answers about myself.'

To get those answers Julie went into five-day-a-week psycho-analysis for the five years, from 1963 to 1968, which represented the peak of her career. 'It is the only decision,' she said, 'that I have ever made, totally, 100 per cent. It was also the wisest.' For years after, she went back to analysts for 'refresher courses'.

Julie's greatest anxiety was the breaking up of her marriage to Tony Walton, her flourishing romance with Blake Edwards, and the effect of both on Emma. 'You have to remember that I came from a broken home,' she said. 'I wondered if I was somehow subconsciously trying to recreate that thing which I had seen happen in my own childhood. And if my parents' divorce had inspired my breakup, would that in turn influence Emma's life?'

'Her divorce caused Julie a great deal of anguish,' her father, Ted Wells, agreed. 'On top of that came the stirrings of unhappiness she had felt when her mother and I parted. It was clear that neither I nor her stepfather had been able to finish off properly the job that a father has to do. One success after another came to Julie, and she never really had time to stop and take a good hard look at herself. Suddenly she needed assurance that the things she believed in were valid. She was also concerned, as any young mother would be, about bring-ing up Emma on her own. Julie knows how shattering a broken marriage can be to a child.'

After *Mary Poppins*, Julie and Tony made an agreement, Tony said, 'never to work on the same thing at the same time. There are enough risks without imposing further ones. If I were to decide to go to Hollywood whatever happened, and be with Julie, it would be a way of being together. But the few times I have been there and not been able to get on with the work that I find satisfying, I've become impossible to be with. And that's as dangerous as not being there at all. Some husbands of stars can fit into the agent-manager role, but I'm not agently inclined and there's pride involved too.'

Rehearsing for a television special with Gene Kelly
1965 NATIONAL BROADCASTING COMPANY

So, when she was making *Hawaii* in Honolulu, he was designing *A Funny Thing Happened on the Way to the Forum* in Spain. When he was doing *The Seagull* in Sweden, she was making *Torn Curtain* and *Thoroughly Modern Millie* in Hollywood. Only *Petulia*, whose location was San Francisco, put him within 'striking distance' of a reconciliation with his wife, but by then, 1967, it was too late.

'We are apart a lot and it is a problem,' she said. 'It's not easy at all. If he were to follow me around and be Mr Julie Andrews, that wouldn't solve anything. We have periods of being enormously lucky, when we can work it out to be together. The rest of the time we have a sort of joint agreement, not to make any demands on the other and a kind of freedom which I find rather marvellous. It isn't easy, especially with Emma. She adores Tony, and one can see why. He is endlessly patient, very kind, a loving father and rock solid.'

Money was still an issue Tony tried to ignore. 'It was mostly pride on my part – no, almost entirely pride,' he said. 'I couldn't conceivably afford the sort of house Julie has in Hollywood, so that sort of expenditure falls entirely on her.' (A house in the tennis town of Wimbledon, where Julie and Tony lived together only a few months, was a joint property. The wind-swept cottage in Alderney was hers.)

One obvious, if extreme, solution would have been for Julie to quit her career. Tony thought that might have been possible only in the first two years of their marriage, 'because we were both in the theatre, and it was never so hard to be together. And she's never been that passionate about the theatre.' But as she became a movie star, she felt that 'to retire would probably lead to a dreadful resentment in me.'

Tony agreed that Hollywood stardom had really involved her for the first time, 'because, despite all her years in the business, this was the first time that she had any real self-confidence, a real feeling that she had a firm grip on things. I don't think she'd like to drop that feeling, not yet anyway. This confidence is the most marvellous and valuable thing

With Leslie Uggams, Miss Piggy and Kermit the Frog,
and Jim Henson 1973

about her success, and I wouldn't want to be responsible for
taking that away from her.'

One of the great strengths of their marriage, Tony felt, had
been that they were each capable of taking the pressure off
the other, particularly when they were both working in the
theatre. 'At times I'd find myself taking on an almost feminine

role, trying to calm, soothe, protect or whatever,' he said. 'And then as soon as I was deeply involved, the roles would be reversed. I think if I were an overly dominant kind of male, I'd find this situation harder to cope with. But neither of us is overpoweringly masculine or feminine, so this switching of roles was a way of making a difficult situation work, but it was hardly the final answer. It's very hard for many women to feel really happy about it. They're grateful that this is possible so that they can work and be independent, but ultimately they resent a man's easing up on his dominance for a second.'

The only time Tony resented being called 'Mr Julie Andrews' was on Alderney, in 1964, at a dinner party. 'A speech was made by someone which referred in a pleasant enough way to "Mr Julie Andrews",' he recalled. 'It got to me like a shot. I don't know why. Maybe because Alderney was such a private, defended place for us.'

In her tapes from Hollywood in 1965 and 1966, Julie kept 'saying how frightened she was of acting, how unreal the whole thing was. But we got too good at the tapes and a bit too tricky,' Tony said. 'Every once in a while I'd get one from Julie saying, "It's midnight and I'm just dragging in from rehearsal," and I could hear the birds singing in the background.'

Early in their marriage Julie had attempted at times to be a traditional wife; not a cook then or ever, she even got his breakfast most mornings. She went with him to Oxford for the opening of the English stage version of *A Funny Thing Happened on the Way to the Forum*. Two women in the foyer of the theatre dimly recognized her face, and one asked: 'Would you mind telling us if you have anything to do with this production?' Julie Andrews smiled and said, 'Certainly. I'm Mrs Walton. My husband designed the scenery.'

But by October of 1966 the Waltons had decided to make their physical separation permanent. Early that month in New York she accompanied him to a preview of the Broadway musical *The Apple Tree*, which he had designed (and which she had turned down, even though her friend Mike Nichols was directing). Tony escorted Julie to the New York première of her *Hawaii* on 10 October. The next day she flew back to Hollywood, work on *Thoroughly Modern Millie*, and Blake Edwards.

Julie's separation from Tony was not a 'trial' separation – there had already been enough trials in separation for that – but it was not a legal separation either, and the Waltons remained legally married for another thirteen months.

'We just decided to try it this way and see what happens,' said Julie. 'The split was not brought on by any one particular rift. There were many reasons – all of them intensely personal. But we have known each other much too long to fight. We are very good friends, as corny as that sounds. He is the best counsel, friend, advisor I have. I really do value his advice more than anyone's. He is one of the biggest influences in my life. I can't put my finger on it exactly, because it's in so many areas. But he's terribly bright, a very intelligent boy. His general help has been fantastic. And his parents are the best bloody in-laws anyone could ever have. They're a family-family – extremely close.'

The Tony Waltons had never been, even at their happiest, the 'family-family' that Julie had craved since infancy, and both she and Tony regretted it, at least on Emma Kate's behalf. He complained that even before the separation he had seen his daughter only about a third of the time she had been alive. 'I've been over-protective about that I know,' Julie admitted. 'But for her to see him would involve some kind of upheaval, a trip to New York or something like that. She talks to him on the phone two or three times a week, and sees him whenever they can get together.'

While Tony held onto the hope of a reconciliation, Julie had postponed their divorce long past the point of any such possibility, thanks to her lifelong ambivalence, and to what her friend Elsie Giorgi called Julie's one 'major fault: she hates to disappoint anyone. As a result she does things that

119

In a television special 1965 NATIONAL BROADCASTING COMPANY

are over-taxing and not even worthy of her. She has a great sense of duty and great conscience. Who else would take two years to say, "We are separated"?'

Mike Nichols had come to Hollywood to direct movies (*Who's Afraid of Virginia Woolf?* and *The Graduate*), and he and Julie saw each other sometimes. While she was making *Torn Curtain* she served as hostess at a party he gave at the Daisy, then the 'in' nightspot in Beverly Hills. Her hairdresser and make-up man from the movie had stayed late in her dressing room that night to prepare her – 'like Cinderella, all fixed up for the party,' she recalled, 'with pants and a big scarf. That's the sort of thing that should happen to you when you're eighteen. I'm thirty.' Guests at the party included Richard Burton and Elizabeth Taylor, Rock Hudson, Lana Turner and Sean Connery, so Julie made news as a hostess and she and Mike Nichols made news as a couple.

Julie would also go out with other men, like Saul Chaplin or Roddy McDowall (who played Mordred in the stage version of *Camelot*), 'Whatever's needed, whenever,' she said. Her father, Ted Wells, came to town, and 'I had a splendid field day with the gossipmongers. I went everywhere, clinging gaily to his arm. I enjoyed thinking what the fan magazines might be making of it.'

Blake Edwards and Julie first met at a party given by Peter Sellers at the Beverly Hills Hotel in 1963, to celebrate the completion of *A Shot in the Dark*, the second of the five Pink Panther movies that Edwards directed, and in which Sellers starred as Inspector Clouseau. 'It was a cursory meeting with just the usual bullshit,' Edwards recalled. 'She said, "I admire your work," and I said, "I admire yours, too."'

They saw each other infrequently after that, at the Goldwyn Studios in Hollywood when she was doing interior scenes for *Hawaii* and he was filming *What Did You Do In The War, Daddy?*, or at parties in the homes of mutual friends. But it was a less than complimentary remark he made one day to a group of men at Goldwyn that really brought Blake and Julie together. He said, offhandedly, that she was 'so sweet she probably has violets between her legs'. When Julie heard about it, she sent Blake a bunch of violets and a note.

Edwards was born in Tulsa, Oklahoma, but was third-generation Hollywood. His grandfather had directed Theda Bara in silent movies, and his father was a production manager. After graduation from Beverly Hills High School and Second World War duty in the Coast Guard, he worked as an actor (playing the local boxing champion who was floored by Cameron Mitchell in Richard Quine's *Leather Gloves*), and sold two scenarios for Westerns. When Dick Powell was looking for a new vehicle, Blake wrote the *Richard Diamond* radio series. From there he moved into writing and directing B movies and television shows; he created *Peter Gunn*. His best work came in the early 1960s, when he directed *Days of Wine and Roses*, *Breakfast at Tiffany's* and *The Pink Panther*.

When he and Julie started seeing one another on a regular basis, his career was in a decline, with his $12-million *The Great Race* selling very few tickets. His fourteen-year marriage to Patricia Walker, a former actress, was ending badly. Julie was ending her marriage slowly, and her career was definitely in the ascendant; she made three major-budget features one after the other, *Hawaii*, *Torn Curtain* and *Thoroughly Modern Millie*.

Edwards lived alone in a large, old-style movie director's house above the Sunset Strip in the hills of West Hollywood, not more than fifteen minutes from Julie's more modest eight-room house off Coldwater Canyon. He was legally separated from his first wife (who lived in London with their children, Jennifer and Geoffrey) and close to a final divorce. His and Julie's first dates were for dinner in public restaurants. They took weekend cruises together, and held hands under the table at a dinner party for eighty at the Bel-Air home of the Anthony Newleys, prompting one observer to sneer: 'She even conducts an affair like Mary Poppins.'

'I had a Rolls-Royce convertible then,' Edwards recalled of their very first date, 'and as we were driving down Sunset Boulevard, I turned to Julie and said, "This is a hell of a way to be anonymous, driving down Sunset Boulevard in an open Rolls-Royce with Mary Poppins!"'

Edwards' separation and divorce had been long in the works, and he was affronted by any suggestion that Julie was a home-wrecker. 'It is as wrong as it can be, and unfair to all concerned, particularly to my wife and children, to say that Julie had anything to do with my marriage breaking up,' he said. 'It was a combination of a lot of things, and my wife and I are trying to organize our separate lives. But that has nothing to do with Julie.'

Before they started going together seriously, Julie and Blake decided to do a picture together – one that he had written. Paramount agreed to assume the production of *Darling Lili* (or *Where Were You on the Night You Said You Shot Down Baron Von Richtofen?*) with her as the title star, and him as director. Blake said, 'While Julie and I are not irrevocably bound together in the deal, we can't really turn back. I think it's risky, our working together, or working with friends in general. I'm determined to keep my personal life apart from my business life, and they inevitably get mixed up if you work with friends. But knowing her and myself at this point, if any two people stand a chance of working together and getting away with it, I'd say we do.'

Blake, who is thirteen years older than Julie, quickly developed total admiration for her, both personally and professionally. 'I feel certain that whatever it is that makes that girl what she is is profound and unique. I told her very early in our friendship that she was an unusual girl. She said, "I'm not, and don't be surprised to find out some day that I'm not." Whatever Julie is does come through on screen. She is an amazingly good actress for my taste. I am startled at times by the honesty of her performance. Now that I know the lady

124

With Leo Sayer on television 1973

from whence it comes, I know that she has an enormous vista yet to tread.'

Through the making of his picture *The Party,* with Peter Sellers, and her *Thoroughly Modern Millie* and *Star!,* their friendship ripened into a fully fledged romance. On 14 November 1967, Julie filed for a California divorce from Tony Walton, on the usual show business grounds of mental cruelty. The 32-year-old actress, who had been living apart from her husband for three years, said in a terse statement: 'The varying demands of our careers have kept Tony and me apart for long periods of time, thus placing obvious strains on our marriage. It has therefore become clear that a divorce would be in the best interests of all concerned.'

Julie and 'Blackie' (so called because of his black sense of humour rather than as a diminutive of Blake) started spending more and more time together, at his new house in Malibu, and with their children in both California and Switzerland, where they began to take winter vacations in 1967. But Julie did not appear to be any more eager to commit herself to a second marriage than she had been to finish the first.

She felt very strongly that it was nobody's business but her own and Blake's (and possibly Emma's and Tony's) how she conducted her private life. 'How dare "they" judge another human being?' she asked of those members of the press and public who turned against movie stars for what they considered public adultery. 'Who knows what goes on in anyone else's life?' Julie decided that 'this hypocrisy is the last dregs of the big-star era, when the public and the press decided how a star should behave.'

Blake agreed with Julie's sentiments about their affair. 'You know that you're going to live your lives the way you want to anyway,' he said, 'but I'm in a better position than she because I'm not a celebrity. The fans and the fan magazines want to know every move she makes, but she is a very bright girl about that. We both feel that they're gonna say what they're gonna say, anyway. You can't avoid that unless you get out of the business.'

'I mostly do what I want to do,' Julie said, 'and don't care what anyone thinks. I do try not to hurt anyone. People will talk and gossip, and there is nothing you can do, so you might just as well go your own sweet way. There is nothing I wish to announce or tell the world. When there is, I will. Until then, I'd rather leave it alone. I don't think anybody goes out of her way to be a scarlet woman, but then there is very little I can do about it if that's what they want to make of it.'

Because she was so totally committed to her career at this point in her life, the mid 1960s, her social and professional lives were hard to separate. Julie once spent an entire evening at a party exacting advice from George Burns; she sat riveted by his explanation of how he and Jack Benny had made their stardoms last a lifetime. Burns told her to embrace all entertainment media. And most of her friends and co-workers attributed Julie's superstardom to the very qualities they found in her as a person.

'I have always felt that this lady was one of the most unusual ladies I've ever been near,' Blake said. 'She has an aura about her that I'm tremendously impressed with. I have a natural ambivalence toward actresses. I usually withdraw from them instinctively at the beginning. They're fine in their place, but I can't have any kind of relationship with them. She's different. She's vitally professional. Her instincts are so damn good. You'll never see her throwing her weight around or being competitive past normal competitiveness, and she seems to be aware of the pitfalls of this business more than most.'

Julie had always played Galatea to a Pygmalion: at first it was her resented stepfather, Ted Andrews; then there came Charles Tucker, Cy Feuer, Moss Hart, Tony Walton and Robert Wise. But Blake Edwards was to become the most influential person in her life, more like Svengali to her Trilby (for several years the pair even considered making a movie called *Trilby*, then they abandoned the idea). But in the early stages of their relationship Blake was still embarked on a search of his own. 'The biggest problem with me,' he said, 'is that there really is no Blake Edwards. I've gone in too many directions so far. Success makes you too aware of the details and apparatus of our business.'

Blake was himself in five-days-a-week psychoanalysis – in his case it lasted for seven years – and he encouraged Julie's sessions with the analyst. She had also been influenced strongly towards it by John Calley and by a London friend, Masud Khan, Svetlana Beriosova's husband, himself a psychiatrist. 'One day I just did it,' Julie recalled. 'I rang up everybody I knew who had a psychiatrist and asked who would be good.'

At first she tried to keep her analysis a secret. Julie told co-workers on *The Sound of Music* and *Hawaii* not to say anything about it, for fear her mother would find out. Eventually, of course, Mrs Andrews did find out, and she pronounced the whole psychiatric profession and Julie's alleged need of its services 'bloody nonsense. You understand, we still looked on them as quacks in England.'

Julie's friend Elsie Giorgi, a medical doctor and dissatisfied subject of analysis, was equally sceptical. 'In analysis she has become a student of it, rather than a patient,' Dr Giorgi said. 'I sometimes wonder who's treating whom. Julie has great intuition, as well as a great intellectual curiosity about everything, and I think this is just one more thing she's learning about.'

But Julie, who had no religious upbringing whatsoever (her only prayers were just before going on stage: 'Oh, God, don't let me fall on my face'), proved to be a zealous convert to psychoanalysis. 'I'm only beginning to crystallize the bits and pieces of my life,' she said, 'and analysis helps. I think I'd have been a rotten mother without analysis. I do have phobias, and there's no doubt about it. I have enormous phobias about singing, stemming from the Broadway days when I was trotted out every night and was pretty much mixed up.

'Some of the neurotic idiosyncracies of worry about my throat during the Broadway run of *My Fair Lady* really hung me up. I was in an absolute tizzy. I got phobias and complexes and everything else. The same was almost true of *Star!* I was on camera constantly for months, and the pressures were enormous. I worried more than I should have.'

Another of her concerns was her tendency to anger, and her expressing it differently from most people. 'I do have a temper, an absolutely fearful one,' she said. 'But I think I am too controlled a human being to let it be said that I have a temper most people would recognize. What usually happens, funnily enough, is that when I'm really blue I get wacky. I'm funniest when things are really down. I do hate scenes of any kind. They upset me desperately, and I go out of my way to avoid them. I used to hate goodbyes to an extent that was ridiculous. I still hate both scenes and goodbyes, but now I know why.'

Both Richard Burton in *Camelot* and Max von Sydow in *Hawaii* saw flashes of her temper, which surprised her because 'I thought I was kidding them the whole time'. Other acquaintances, like actress Tammy Grimes, wished Julie would show her temper and her other feelings a bit more. 'She's sad and boring,' said Grimes, 'she's lost Eliza. Her accent is too high. She does just what's right. It would be groovier if she'd do just what's Julie once in a while.'

Ambivalence, Julie felt, was 'another of my failings. Ambivalence can either be a vice or a virtue. But I am able to see both sides of anything to such an extent that it is terribly hard for me to make a decision or do anything involving a drastic change. My kind of temper, when it does come out, is a stewing kind. I grit my teeth at the things that really do get me upset and I simmer for a while. It's the little things that get me mad. I'm terribly good about coping with big problems. One of my ambitions used to be to throw a great screaming temper tantrum. I can't see myself actually doing it, but I have fantasized it. To do it you have to be pretty damn sure that you're right or you look damn foolish. And because I'm totally ambivalent, I'm never that sure.'

But the biggest phobia of all proved to be her fear of success, or at least her failure to understand why it was happening to her so fast. 'You have this panic, this weight,' Julie said. 'You cope with it day by day, and sometimes everything is chaotic on the surface. I need order – desperately – but I can't have it. And there's never any time. Then there is this very great loneliness. It is hard, the pressure; often I get headaches. But one hopes it is not for nothing.'

8

JERUSHA AND MILLIE

WITH *The Sound of Music* secure as the new box office champion of the world, and an Oscar to certify her acting ability, Julie's only professional problem was 'that I'll be considered the nanny of all time'. There was nothing to do but marry Jesus in New England and go to Hawaii on a long honeymoon – and do it all for a real movie-star price, $400,000.

Max von Sydow, the Swedish actor who had played Christ in George Stevens's *The Greatest Story Ever Told*, was cast as a Fundamentalist missionary who hopes to convert the Polynesian natives in Hawaii to Christianity, in the film *Hawaii*. Julie was cast as his unwilling wife by an arranged marriage, Jerusha. The story, based on a third of James Michener's rambling novel of the same name, appealed to Julie, who was anxious to try another straight, non-musical character.

'Oh, marvellous publicity – can't you see it?' she chortled just before the start of shooting. 'Mary Poppins married Jesus. Gorgeous! She must have flown up to him and said,

"Listen, with my magic and your talent, we'd make a great team. I can fly. You can walk on water. What more do we need?" Actually, come to think of it, who else could Mary Poppins have married? It's the classic mother and father image for our children.'

There was less to laugh at once *Hawaii* was actually under way. Shooting started in Sturbridge Village, a reconstructed colonial town in south-western Massachusetts. The stars couldn't get to the location sight because the spring snow in New England had stopped all air traffic, so they were driven up from New York in a chauffeur-driven limousine. Once in Sturbridge, a paid-admission park which had been rented to play the part of Walpole, New Hampshire, of one hundred and forty years before, Julie learned for the first time the real meaning of the word 'superstar'.

'That little place, that's where she learned what she was,' said William 'Daddy Bill' Buell, Julie's long-time make-up man. Prior to *Hawaii*, there had been a few incidents, mostly in department stores when Julie was shopping, or with mothers poking their children and saying, 'Look, dear, there's Mary Poppins!' But in Sturbridge mob hysteria took over.

'People started to converge as I was walking to my trailer,' Julie recalled. 'These very sizeable, nice policemen were around me, and people would be on one side being pushed back by the husky policemen, and then they would circle around and come in from the other side. You could hear them saying, "Look, it's Mary Poppins," to their children. They didn't mean any harm, it was a lark for them. But then I got into my trailer and I was alone in eight square feet of space, alone in this island. You could hear them outside giggling and joshing and pushing. And the trailer was swaying. They were scratching at the walls. I pulled down the shades and sat there alone. I thought, "My God, how alone I am. I can't send for anybody. I can't get out."''

Whenever and wherever she went to eat around Sturbridge, she was mobbed by adoring fans. For a weekend sightseeing trip with a friend from New York, she requested a small, older-model car so that the two of them could go sightseeing unrecognized. The move worked. On another occasion, a zealous fan managed to steal a costume bonnet from her trailer dressing room. From Sturbridge, the *Hawaii* company went back to Hollywood to shoot some interiors, and then on to the Kahala section of Honolulu, where Julie, von Sydow, and director George Roy Hill all had large houses. Unusually, this picture was filmed more or less chronologically, from von Sydow's graduation from divinity school in New Hampshire to his marriage, to on board ship to Hawaii, to the arrival in the Islands, and straight through to twenty years later.

'I fell in love with Hawaii,' Julie said. 'There had been Sturbridge, all cool and New Englandish, and then there was Hawaii – it was quite a change. To watch the dawn in those islands is one of the memorable experiences of a lifetime. Hawaii is gorgeous and fabulous. Where else could you drive up to a roadstand and get a paper plate with hamburger, French fries, mustard, and an orchid?'

Julie became so infatuated with Hawaii that she bought an interest in a macadamia nut orchard and returned to the islands frequently in later years for vacations. Emma Kate stayed with Julie at the Kahala house 'every moment of the time', along with her nanny and Julie's half-brother Christopher. Julie screened movies at her home, including Godard's *Breathless*, and she gave parties, including one for all the nannies, tutors and other household help in the company. When she had time off during the day she often relaxed alone on a secluded beach near the set, in a bikini.

'Although I loved the islands unashamedly,' Julie remembered, 'it was ten times harder working there, and six months was too long.' In particular, she remembered hot and long, uncomfortable days on the Oahu beaches and three weeks offshore on the 150-ton schooner, filming the sea voyage scenes.

The $12-million picture was falling badly behind schedule, so studio executives flew out from Hollywood. They found director Hill spending most of his time working with the Polynesians, most of whom were totally untrained as actors but crucial to the action. Julie felt that she was not getting enough of the director's attention, and Hill was fired by producer Walter Mirisch. Julie acquiesed in the firing by staying silent.

The Polynesians, led by Jocelyne La Garde, a French-speaking Tahitian standing six feet tall and weighing 300 pounds, who was making her acting debut as Malama, the Polynesian queen, (so effectively that she got an Oscar nomination), and Manu Tupou, who played her consort, went on strike until Hill was reinstated. Julie thought La Garde and Tupou 'had their nerve' refusing to work, and she would have no part in it. But once Hill was back on the picture, he and Julie became such good friends that she asked him to direct *Thoroughly Modern Millie*.

Another irony of the situation was that Hill had fought to cast Julie as Jerusha in the first place. 'It's awfully hard to get a girl who can play a convincing young lady of breeding of the 1820s in New England,' Hill explained. 'What other names spring to mind? People of the 1820s – particularly in New England – were closer to the lands of their birth than to the Americans of today. There was a great stillness in the people of that time. That is what I tried to get, and that is what Julie has. She is reserved, yet warm and aristocratic.'

'At first I thought I was miscast as the missionary's wife,' Julie countered. 'I didn't think I was in total sympathy with the lady. I wasn't as subdued as she was. My personality is more bubbly. And I felt I wasn't doing anything, just repressing myself and being her. I had never met anyone like Jerusha. She left her home, turned away from the man she really loved to stay with a husband she didn't love, to suffer the hardships and deprivations of a missionary's wife on an untamed island. I don't think I would have done that. But

With von Sydow in *Hawaii* 1966

George was patient with me, Max was lovely and a marvellous actor to work with, and finally I loved the work and the part.'

Shortly after she arrived in Honolulu, Julie went to visit the wax museum, 'and I almost dropped in my tracks. There was a wax figure of the first lady missionary in Hawaii, and if that lady isn't the very image of me! I had an eerie feeling that I was destined by fate for this part.'

Julie's most important scene in *Hawaii* was the one in which she gave birth to a child. It was shot in the converted Navy warehouse in Honolulu that was serving as a studio, and it took seventeen hours over a period of six days. 'All I produced was a lump of celluloid,' she said. 'But I don't think I could have done the scene without having had a baby myself. There was a real doctor counselling on the set, and after every take he would put his hand on my head and ask if I felt all right, just as if I *were* having a baby. Opening night in New York, I noticed that women were fastened on the screen during that scene. The men, I think, rather didn't like it.'

The scene that everyone else had trouble with, Julie found easy. Warned to 'dose up' before she shot the storm at sea, 'I ate nine pancakes for ballast, took six Dramamines and belted down a large scotch. I was so drunk I was the only one who wasn't sick.'

Richard Harris, who played Jerusha's spurned lover, Max von Sydow, and Julie gave the cast a dinner party at the Kahala Hilton Hotel. Don Ho was brought in to sing. He and Julie did a duet of his hit 'I'll Remember You', with Julie repeating each verse as he sang it, because she didn't know the words. Asked to sing a solo, she said, 'I'm sorry, but of all the songs I've sung the only one I can remember all the words to is "I Could Have Danced All Night".' So she sang that song from *My Fair Lady* to the aloha-shirted and muumuu-ed crowd, and nothing else.

During *Hawaii*, Julie developed two satisfying professional relationships, one with Hill, and the second with von Sydow. The Swedish star was her favourite leading man, she said,

'The unqualified front-runner, the most generous man I've ever met, with a light, lovely sense of humour.'

Von Sydow found that Julie 'made fun of herself and her part in a marvellous way, and yet she is so god-damned professional even in the most difficult situations. She doesn't behave like the cliché star. She has a temper, but she is also a disciplined lady, and does not use her temper just because she feels like it. She is nice with people, but she is determined to do things right, and she will stick up for what she thinks is right. She doesn't show off.

'I learned a lot from her about movie discipline. I have a tendency to tenseness all day when I'm on a picture, to stay with my part the whole time – which made me too exhausted too early in the day. She, on the other hand, has a great ability to walk into a part and then out of it again, to do her part one minute and then relax the next – to do other things, write letters, see people, listen to music, sing and laugh, and then go right back to being Jerusha.'

When the film opened, critics were kinder to her than to the film, which bogged down in slow pacing and epic length. Her father, Ted Wells, said *Hawaii* convinced him for the first time that his daughter could act as well as sing. Of her own efforts in *Hawaii*, Julie said, 'I did have reservations about myself – one always does – but I do like little bits that I did. *Hawaii* was rewarded with eight Academy Award nominations, basically for its big effort. All but La Garde's nomination were in technical categories, and the film won no Oscars.

With barely a week in between, Julie went from Honolulu and *Hawaii* to Hollywood for *Torn Curtain*, the spy picture that was to be Alfred Hitchcock's fiftieth film. Julie had hated the script, but her agents had convinced her that working with Hitchcock and co-star Paul Newman would be the best (meaning the most lucrative) thing that she could do at that moment. Because she wanted to work with those two men, she agreed, and plunged ahead with the picture despite a severe case of fatigue from *Hawaii*.

Torn Curtain had waited for her return from the islands, so when production started in November of 1965, the movie was already behind schedule. The setting of the story was Copenhagen and East Berlin, but all shooting involving the two stars took place entirely on the Universal back lot – and it looked it. Although it was not a big budget film, what money was spent (about $5 million) went to Hitchcock's and to the stars' salaries – Julie got $750,000 against 10 per cent of the gross, more than Newman, who was nonetheless billed first – and not to production values. Perhaps that was why everybody, including Hitchcock, seemed to walk through *Torn Curtain*.

For the first time in her life on stage or screen, Julie was playing a contemporary woman, Sarah Sherman, secretary-mistress to an American scientist (Newman), who has supposedly defected to the Communists. She stubbornly follows him from Copenhagen to Berlin, although he has told her not to complicate both their lives by doing so. The movie opens with Julie and Newman, who are not married and not contemplating it, in bed together, albeit far from nude.

This was a shock to many admirers of the Mary Poppins image, and entirely unacceptable to the National Roman Catholic Office for Motion Pictures, the successor to the Legion of Decency, which condemned the picture as 'morally objectionable in part or all', for its 'gratuitous introduction of pre-marital sex between its sympathetic protagonists'. The Catholic Office also said that the movie's 'detailed treatment of a realistically brutal killing [was] questionable on moral grounds', and concluded with a warning: 'Parents should be aware that the "Mary Poppins" image of the female lead (Julie Andrews), shattered in this film, can not serve as any criterion of the film's acceptability for their children.'

Julie, of course, took a different view. 'As it was necessary to the story to establish our close relationship, I saw no harm in it,' she said. 'Paul Newman was such a nice man; we didn't take it seriously, and had a lot of giggles over it. It didn't last

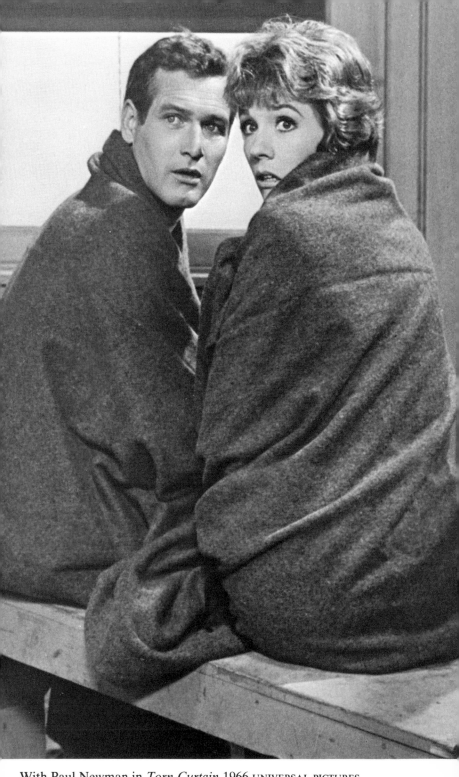

With Paul Newman in *Torn Curtain* 1966 UNIVERSAL PICTURES

long, so I don't see what all the fuss is about. I prefer to be known as an actress, not an image.'

Making *Torn Curtain* did not provide either the fun or the professional satisfaction that Julie's four previous movies had. On the set, Newman was nice (he called her 'the last of the really great dames'), but there wasn't a close friendship between them. Even Julie's clowning on the set of *Torn Curtain* was more forced and less funny than before.

When Hitchcock complained at one point of a spotlight 'making a hell of a line over her head', she demurely put her hands on her hips and said, 'That's my halo.' Another day she was lying on the bed in what was supposed to be her Copenhagen hotel room, and suddenly she said to the director, 'Won't the camera be looking up my skirt?' Newman squatted down next to the camera and looked. 'Yeah, that's the idea,' he said. 'Oh, you beastly thing,' she retorted. 'I say, did you see the cartoon about Mary Poppins? She is sailing through the air with her umbrella, and there are two little boys on the ground looking up. One of them says, "Coo, you can see right up her skirt."' Everybody on the set laughed, but dutifully rather than heartily.

That three well-known perfectionists like Alfred Hitchock, Paul Newman, and Julie Andrews could have made the slipshod bundle of clichés that *Torn Curtain* became was a minor wonder. That the movie made money on its initial release in the summer of 1966 was a major miracle, but a tribute to all three names and their combined potency at the box office, despite the critics' justifiably acid reviews.

Julie was privately so upset by the final result that she urged her good friends not to see *Torn Curtain*. Even publicly, though she tried to be discreet, some of her resentment over the experience came through. 'I did not have to act in *Torn Curtain*,' she said. 'I merely went along for the ride. I don't feel that the part demanded much of me – other than to look glamorous, which Mr Hitchcock can always arrange better than anyone. I did have reservations about the film, but I

Beatrice Lillie, Carol Channing, Julie Andrews, Mary Tyler Moore, James Fox and John Gavin in a cast line-up for *Thoroughly Modern Millie* 1966 UNIVERSAL PICTURES

wasn't agonized by it. The kick of it was working for Hitchcock. That's what I did it for, and that's what I got out of it. So that's that.'

Ross Hunter, the Universal producer, wanted to do the film version of *The Boy Friend*, with Julie recreating her lead role as Polly Browne, but the property was owned by Metro-Goldwyn-Mayer, who wouldn't sell it. So Hunter decided instead to make *Thoroughly Modern Millie*, which was first conceived as a comedy about a young career girl in New York in the 1920s, and not as a musical.

'I read the script as a favour to Ross Hunter,' Julie said. 'I thought it would be the last chance I'd have to do the ingenue.

After all, when you're thirty-two, how many more chances can you have? It was my last fling at a part like that.'

She was so enthusiastic about the concept that she cancelled a vacation, and put off all other pictures, including *Star!*, to do *Thoroughly Modern Millie*. Julie got Hunter to hire George Roy Hill, who worked with scriptwriter Richard Morris on the conversion of the screenplay to a musical. Sammy Cahn and Jimmy Van Heusen wrote four new songs, including the title number, and Mary Tyler Moore, Carol Channing, James Fox, and Beatrice Lillie were signed to play supporting roles. The budget was boosted to $8 million.

Julie found herself 'very excited about *Millie*; it had great style, it was wild and wacky, it had a marvellous cast. The way the script was written, the character walked a fine line between a selfish, tough, ambitious girl and a fine lady. The challenge was to be that whole person. I hope one didn't fall one way or t'other. The picture was *very* twenties – high style, but not high camp.'

Ross Hunter claimed to have found 'a new Julie. She had a lot of sex appeal and a clean look. I've never worked with anyone like her, and I've worked with them all. She is probably one of the greatest stars ever in the business.'

She did not stint on the help she gave her co-stars, and one day when she was not needed on the set at all Julie came in to read her lines off camera for Carol Channing to react, instead of having her stand-in do it. Hunter and Channing were both flabbergasted. 'I've never had anyone help me the way Julie did,' said Carol. 'That would be unheard of for any other star,' said Hunter.

Channing told Julie after the incident, 'If it had been your stand-in, I wouldn't have spoken the same way to her.'

Julie said, 'Yes, I knew that, that's why I'm here.'

'I always play to Julie,' said Carol. 'She was the one who was listening. She grabbed the words right out of my mouth.'

When Channing lost her *Hello, Dolly!* role to Barbra Streisand for the movie version (as she had lost *Gentlemen*

With Beatrice Lillie in *Thoroughly Modern Millie*
1967 UNIVERSAL PICTURES

Prefer Blondes to Marilyn Monroe), Julie wired her: 'Don't worry, Carol, you'll get your *Mary Poppins*.'

'Now wasn't that just the right thing to say?' said Carol.

But Channing was more impressed with Julie's determination than with her sweetness. 'With Julie it's not "Who loves me? How sweet am I? Do you think I'm dear?" and all that sort of stuff. Instead it's work, work, work. She's completely career, and businesslike. She's all for the goal, and it doesn't matter if she's subtle about it – and to me that's the most feminine thing there is. She's dead-on honest. What she wants is ability around her; it makes her better. If you have that ability, or can develop it, she's all with you.

'There was a fly on the set during one close-up,' Channing remembered. 'Julie jumped up and said, "Well, we are going to get that fly, damn it, we are going to get it." The director had a fly-swatter, and he was just going to swat it when she grabbed it out of his hand and swatted the fly and killed it. Now, you know you can't do that to a man, and I laughed and said, "Julie, honey, you are the kind of woman who pushes the elevator button first when you are standing there with a man," and she said, "Why not, for heaven's sake?"'

George Roy Hill, directing his second movie with Julie and not emasculated by the loss of his fly-swatter, said of his star: 'There was a period when she seemed a little too good to be true, but she has at last gone beyond that. If I had searched the earth for a different movie for Julie after *Hawaii*, I couldn't have come up with a better one than *Millie*. Jerusha was subdued by nature. Millie was so alive that Julie came in every day with a thousand ideas of what to do. She fell completely into the style of the picture and was great fun on the set. We were hysterical and helpless with laughter most of the time.'

Universal executives took one look at the rough-cut footage of *Millie* that Ross Hunter showed them and decided that the picture should be shown in 70mm as a reserve-seat attraction for Easter in New York and summer in London, Los Angeles, and the rest of the world. To be this kind of road show, long enough for an intermission and to allow high ticket prices, almost all the footage shot would have to be left in the movie. Julie and Hill were distressed by this decision, thinking that they had a very good – possibly even great – 'little' picture on their hands. She made a list of seventy grievances, mostly having to do with length, and pleaded with Universal to cut the film (particularly the gratuitous Jewish wedding song 'Trinkt Lechaim', which had been nothing more than a cynical sop to the Jewish theatre party and matinée audience.

Julie's pressing to release *Thoroughly Modern Millie* as a regular movie was based on artistic considerations, but Lew Wasserman, president of MCA, which owned Universal, saw a chance to cash in on the current popularity of both road shows and Julie Andrews. They made none of her cuts, and that left her cool to Universal. 'Their way, it was blown up too far out of proportion from its original conception,' she said. But MCA was proved right when the picture was released as a long film and broke *Torn Curtain*'s record for the top grosser for Universal. But *Millie* also established Andrews, temporarily, as the only star who could guarantee the success of a movie. (The Burtons proved they could make a pretty good movie do even better, but they couldn't save a true turkey).

Just after *Millie* was made, but months before it was released, casting began at Warner Brothers for the screen version of *Camelot*. Jack Warner was personally producing the film, as he had *My Fair Lady*, and he let it be known that he would like Julie to recreate Guinevere in the film – a tacit admission that he had made a mistake the first time around. Her agent said that Julie would be interested in the movie, and Warner Brothers promised to send her a script. But Richard Burton, who had also been approached to re-do King Arthur, was working in a succession of pictures with his wife Elizabeth Taylor and was not really interested in *Camelot*. Stories circulated that Julie was asking as much as $1,200,000, just to get even with Jack Warner, but it was doubtful that negotiations ever got that far.

145

Warners instead signed Richard Harris and Vanessa Redgrave as King Arthur and Queen Guinevere. Director Joshua Logan was not in the majority of those who felt that Julie Andrews was right for the screen version of any musical that came along, even *Mame*. He was delighted with Redgrave, who herself said, 'I'm sure if Julie Andrews wanted to play this part, she'd be playing it.'

But Logan, who, with Alan Jay Lerner, had completely overhauled the conception of *Camelot* in its transition from stage to screen, asked in a sneering tone, 'Can you see two men and two armies going to war over Julie Andrews?'

9

MUMMY

THE role Julie really liked – and played – best was that of Mum. 'She feels safer with her baby,' said Tammy Grimes. 'She becomes all warm and kind of mummy.'

Particularly after she finished her second three movies in a row, Julie tried to arrange to be at home with Emma Kate in the late afternoons and evenings, and on weekends. For this reason she preferred to continue working in movies rather than even considering any offers to go back on stage. Julie guarded Emma's privacy obsessively, never telling the names of the schools she attended for fear of kidnapping. And from the time her daughter was eighteen months old until she was six, Julie forbade pictures to be taken of herself alone with Emma.

She was so jealous of her own time with her daughter that even when she dutifully delivered Emma to Tony Walton in New York for a few days' visit, she would reserve the important days – like Emma's birthday and Christmas – for herself. When Emma was in nursery school, five mornings a week

Julie drove her there and picked her up in a black 1965 Ford Falcon with simulated wood sides and a *Mary Poppins is a Junkie* bumper-sticker that Mike Nichols had given her. 'Julie drove up to the school just like all the other mothers,' said her business manager Guy Gadbois, 'slightly apologetic about being there.'

Emma, a blue-eyed blonde who actually looked more like her father, had a short hair-do like her mother's and shared some of her mannerisms, and many of her interests. Like Julie, Emma would go around the house whistling, and singing in a modified British accent. When Julie took up oil painting in the summer of 1966, Emma emulated her, and the four-year-old was likely to be seated right alongside her mother in their poolhouse with her little box of watercolours. Once, when Julie had an interview at home, Emma, then six years old, sat quietly in the living room with a sheath of paper in her lap. Julie asked her what she was doing. 'I'm having an interview, too, Mummy,' was the answer.

During the high-pressure movie period of the mid 1960s, Emma loved to watch her mother on the screen – and sometimes would even greet her in real life with 'Hi, Julie Andrews!' The three musicals were shown to Emma first; *The Americanization of Emily* and *Torn Curtain* were withheld from her for a few years. Julie let her see *Hawaii* half at a time – 'Not that I think she couldn't take it all, but she might fall asleep, and then I'd be terribly embarrassed.'

Emma liked to be sung asleep by Julie, 'But she hated for me to *practise* singing,' her mother said about the heavily musical period stretching from *Thoroughly Modern Millie* to *Star!* and including a Christmas album that Julie recorded with André Previn in 1966. 'She would burst into real tears whenever I practised, shouting, "Stop it; I don't want you to do it." She kept trying bravely to conquer it. One day André and I were practising at home, and Emma came in. She said, "Mummy, if I sit very quietly may I watch?", which she never would have thought to ask before. She sat for a few minutes, looking very uncomfortable, and then asked to leave the room. She had heard all she could stand.'

Since Emma was not yet five during that period, she took a nap in the early afternoons, well within range of the pool-house where Julie practised, making it somewhat difficult for Julie to rehearse her songs. 'The only time I could do it was driving to the studio early in the morning. There I was, driving down Coldwater Canyon, clinging to the wheel for dear life, completely oblivious to everything around me, singing at the top of my lungs. I'm sure when I pulled up to a light the person in the next car thought to himself, "Now, who's that crazy woman?'

If Emma missed her father, she filled in by 'clinging to my brother Chris', said Julie. Chris Andrews, Julie's younger half-brother, first lived with Julie and Emma in Hawaii, and then in California while he studied photography at the Art Centre school in Los Angeles. He was twenty when he arrived at the Beverly Hills house in 1966. He took over the bedroom that the butler had once occupied.

Other members of the household at the time included two dogs and a cat. The dogs, an almost-white toy poodle named Q-Tip ('Because he looks like a used one,' Julie explained), and a black standard poodle named Cobie lived in harmony with the grey-and-white cat named Bimbo. Emma romped regularly with the three animals, but Julie gave them scant attention.

The house was still in the firm charge of the butler Covington, called Cov by his mistress, who did most of the cooking and answered the door and the telephone. A laundress came in most days and doubled as a babysitter when the nanny was away. Julie had a full-time secretary, with whom she worked three days a week at home or on the movie set, and two days a week at the secretary's home. When the kitchen was being remodelled and Covington was away doing Army duty, Julie, who was 'hopeless' in the kitchen anyway, and Emma had their suppers at the local Hamburger Hamlet.

149

Given her nomadic early existence, brought on first by the War and divorce, then by show business, it wasn't surprising that Julie had long sought a place to call home. What was surprising was that this typically English girl found it in Southern California. Julie had first 'fallen in love with it' on her honeymoon with Tony in 1959. When she returned four years later to work in *Mary Poppins* she told Carol Burnett that 'she'd never been happier anyplace.'

'Having bought this house has made me feel truly at home here in Hollywood,' she said. 'When I first came I put it down like everyone else, and said that there was nothing going on here. I didn't know a soul when I arrived. I hated the fact that I had to drive everywhere. But now I think that Hollywood is as real as New York or as real as London or as real as Venice. But to really appreciate it, you must go away and come back again. Sometimes when I feel lonely or depressed, it helps me to think that Venice *is* at that moment – that Rome is teeming. It keeps one from being too isolated.'

The modern white-brick, wood, and glass house was plunked onto a private hillside. It was in a corner of Coldwater Canyon known as Hidden Valley, and it was ideally located about fifteen or twenty minutes from all Hollywood movie studios and about twenty minutes from downtown Beverly Hills. Despite its central location, it was in semi-wild canyon country, and had the feeling of being totally isolated – and it was way off the routes of the sightseeing buses that visited stars' homes. Julie preferred it that way. 'I like being out of doors, and I like the country better than the city. My real Dad taught me to love the country. The only salvation for an apartment in London or New York is if you can see trees, a park, or a river.'

The pool and the poolhouse were across the driveway from the house, and beyond them was an extra lot containing Emma's playground (swings, see-saw, and slide). The property was ringed by pear, apple, and avocado trees, and wild canyon plants. In front of the house was a flagstone courtyard,

With Blake Edwards 1981

with a fountain which was lighted at night. At the back of the house, in the best Californian tradition, was an eating patio.

Julie had fireplaces in both her living and dining rooms, and she installed one in her huge bedroom (the whole upstairs of the house). Because Julie thought she was in her house to stay she completely re-did the kitchen, and had an adjacent sun porch converted to a family breakfast room. Central air-conditioning was installed, and all the oak parquet floors were stained dark. Bougainvillea bushes were added to the garden she inherited.

The furnishings in the house ran to elegant things like white Wedgwood bone china. There was a Grotian Steinmeg grand piano at one end of the living room, under a straight open staircase leading down from the bedroom. Behind the staircase was a glass wall facing south, allowing the room to be filled with sunlight for most of the day. In this room was most of Julie's art collection, which she planned to expand. There were two bronzes by Anna Mahler, daughter of the composer Gustav, and a friend of Julie's: a highly unsuccessful head of Julie, and a delicate, graceful, three-foot-high statue of an anonymous girl. She also had a Gyneth Johnstone Italian landscape, an African fertility doll, and five oil paintings by the Oakland, California, artist Henrietta Berk. Blake Edwards, who had several Berks of his own, introduced Julie to the artist's works – semi-abstracts of flowers, children, trees, oceans, and fields in bright warm reds, oranges, blues and greens.

Julie and André Previn played a favourite paintings game: 'If you could buy any five paintings in the world for yourself, what would they be?' explained Previn. 'I played it with Julie one afternoon, not limiting her to five, and she chose "Anything by Turner, but that really is day-dreaming – that's just for the game – and any of the strange, wonderful birds and winged creatures by Braque, and anything by Manet, Monet, Pissarro, Sisley – especially *The Canal, The Woodcutter*, and *The Orchard* – Daumier (titled *The Refugees*) and any still-life by Redon, like *Bouquet of Wild Flowers,* and any of Nolde's watercolours."'

'The trouble is one wants so much,' Julie said, and she seemed reluctant to buy herself even one major painting for each of her movies. Her business manager Guy Gadbois said she wasn't earning enough to buy what were then $30,000 pictures. While she agreed with Gadbois about her own art collection, she weakened where Blake was concerned. For Christmas 1967 she gave him Emil Nolde's *The Singer* ('Somewhat appropriate, I thought'), and for his birthday in 1968 she gave him a Persian waterjug from 1000 BC that she had acquired in Brussels while they were making *Darling Lili.*

Ted Wells had raised his daughter on *The Oxford Book of English Verse* and *The Golden Treasury*, and as a single parent raising her daughter, Julie found herself reading

With Blake's daughter, Jennifer, during filming of
Darling Lili on location in Eire 1968

poetry again. 'When I'm very busy, it's hard to get into a deep novel. But you can pick up a book of poems and read as much as your heart desires. I go off into another world.' Her favourite poet was Robert Frost, for his simplicity and sense of nature.

Recorded classical music was another important part of Julie's home life. 'Whenever I call her or go over there, the record player is going,' said André Previn, 'and it is not for my benefit. She really knows music and loves it.' Svetlana Beriosova agreed that Julie had 'great love and understanding of music and dance. I visited her in California when she was in the midst of *Mary Poppins*, and one night we just sat listening to Benjamin Britten's *War Requiem* and ended up hearing it twice.'

153

Julie's stardom made it hard for her to go out in public at this point. 'Going anywhere with her was a little like blockade-running,' said André Previn. But it also gave her access to any studio's current movies to screen at home. 'I screen the movies on the smooth wall of the playroom if it's a good movie,' she explained, 'on the brick of the living room if it's a bad movie.'

When she went out, it was usually to small dinner parties, escorted by Blake Edwards. She never drank more than a glass of wine. 'I'm too cautious, too careful a person,' Julie explained, 'I'd be terrified of what I'd reveal if I ever really let go.' Nonetheless, her only two 'culinary' specialities were alcoholic drinks. 'She makes the best bullshots in the world,' said Carol Burnett. 'I always think, soup and liquor, so good for you.'

'And every Christmas,' said Julie, 'to everyone's annoyance and chagrin, I make mulled wine, all icky and sticky. I'm the only one who likes it.'

In small groups Julie was both her wittiest and most enigmatic. 'She had a far-out sense of humour,' said Previn. 'She loves to be the clown, and is much more broadly amusing than one would suspect. She is not above saying things you could not say on a movie screen. I don't know why she is such a reserved lady or seems so, but while she's saying all these things and while she's at her funniest, you're never quite sure what she's thinking.'

At home Julie 'always' wore slacks and simple blouses or sweaters, and she often wore the same outfit to work. An admirer of simplicity, she had only four pieces of jewellry 'that I wear off and on'. She wore a plain watch with a plain black strap and, of course, no engagement or wedding ring. For the Hollywood première of *Hawaii* she borrowed a diamond brooch. After *Star!* and the influence of Gertrude Lawrence's ghost, Julie's taste ran to more jewellery on glamorous occasions, but during the day, at home and work, she wore none.

Her taste in clothes for more public occasions was both old-fashioned and frumpish, and she belied the contemporary mid 1960s English 'mod' movement. At one Hollywood party, she arrived 'looking like the chaperone', according to André Previn. 'She didn't act it, but she looked it. She was younger than most of the other guests there, but she looked older.' Tammy Grimes, who also attended the same party, a sit-down dinner with live rock-band dancing afterward, said: 'She wore white gloves. I thought the press was going to come and give her an award.'

'I don't deny that I adore clothes,' said Julie. 'My greatest pleasure is picking out a new gown. I used to be influenced a lot by Tony. I used to wear a lot of black for some sombre reason, until he informed me rather tartly one day that black made my skin look all blotchy.'

Tony Walton recalled that Julie had 'little interest in the business side of her career and always found it difficult to discuss money'. But Gadbois disagreed. 'She has a good awareness of her business affairs,' he said. 'She is a very conservative person who wants to know what's going on all the time, and she's very inquisitive about where her money's going.' Julie's and Gadbois' major disagreement was over a Mercedes she wanted and eventually got. But he urged her to make do with the 1965 Falcon with a new set of tyres for a while longer, and she did.

Her investments, he said, 'are of a conservative nature, conservatively diversified'. Julie and Gadbois discussed every major expenditure, and they met once a week to discuss business. He took care of all household expenses, based on a budget that Julie had approved. She had a small allowance for very personal expenses. 'It's her own money, and if she wants something badly enough she'll get it,' said Gadbois. 'But Julie's sensible enough to know that we're right about the art collection.'

Julie's only work during the time off between the finish of *Thoroughly Modern Millie* and the start of *Star!* was recording the Christmas album with André Previn, who had also conducted the musical numbers for *Millie*. Recordings were a medium Julie had tried to embrace, but she was inexplicably unsuccessful at selling albums other than the sound-track of *The Sound of Music* and the original cast of *My Fair Lady*, which were then the two best-selling albums of all time. Her solo collections of songs in the late 1950s and 1960s did not do well and prevented her from making more albums later on. So *A Christmas Treasure* in 1967 proved to be her last original album other than movie sound-tracks (though some of her earlier records were re-released in the 1970s). It bothered Julie not to succeed in this one medium, especially since she considered herself primarily a singer and had had such fantastic success on stage, in movies and television. She envied Barbra Streisand's making it in those three media and with records as well.

One problem may have been that Julie abhored recording sessions until the one with Previn. 'I admire his quiet affirmation that all is right,' she said. 'In one of the orchestrations on the Christmas album there was a top G at the end, and I hadn't sung a top G since "I Could Have Danced All Night". He said I could do it, and I did it.'

Some of the old Christmas carols they did were on odd clefs, but Previn said, 'I really think after one hearing she had two-thirds of it down cold. She evidently has instant retention for music. Working with her you find out why she made it so big. Singers are generally a dangerous, unpredictable lot. But Julie comes to any session completely prepared and knowing exactly what to do. She is totally willing to take suggestions, but I don't mean everybody can walk all over her. She is a very good singer who acts rather than a movie star who sings.'

Emma Kate increasingly showed creative tendencies, mainly by painting and making up clever word-images. 'She's a worse romantic than I am,' her mother said. 'I wouldn't mind her being an actress if that's what she wants some day; I don't think I could stop her if I tried.' Julie was determined

156

With Blake on location for *Darling Lili*
1968 PARAMOUNT PICTURES

that if Emma did want a career in entertainment, she would
have all the dancing and drama lessons her mother never had
and now sorely missed. One of Emma's favourite stuffed toys
epitomized her daughter's character, in Julie's opinion. It was
a white-and-purple fabric hippopotamus, about a foot long,

around whose neck Emma had placed a dog's collar and leash. 'That's my daughter,' said Julie, 'one day she'll put a leash on a hippopotamus.'

Happy as Julie and Emma were in California, there were times when Julie became nostalgic for her old house in Walton-on-Thames. And she regretted that she seldom got to her cottage on Alderney, in the Channel Islands. (Her father looked after it, supervising its use by any members of her family who cared to stay there.) 'I never intend to lose the cottage,' she said. 'It's sweet and small. Alderney is small enough and wild enough and free enough to be totally removed. For the first few days you damn near die and say, "Oh, I'll never stand all this wind through me," but it's such a totally fresh climate that you never want to leave, and when you do you're completely exhilarated.'

Christmas time in particular made Julie long for some colder weather than that in California. Beginning in 1967 she and Blake and Emma would go to Gstaad, Switzerland, for the holidays. Blake's children, Jennifer and Geoffrey, joined them from London and Julie's maternal instincts quickly broadened to include them. Jenny and Geoffrey were five and three years older than Emma Kate, and they called their father's friend Julie almost from first meeting. Jennifer particularly responded to Julie as she might to an older sister or youngish aunt. On the *Darling Lili* locations in France and Ireland Jenny and Julie sang a song about their expanded 'family' that they had made up, to the tune of 'My Favourite Things'; it began with 'Blackie and Julie and Jenny and Geofrey/Emma and . . .' and extended on to include half-brothers and sisters. For Julie it was the beginning of the big, happy, family unit she had longed for. Then the biggest, best-paid movie star in the world, she said, 'Emma Kate is my greatest production and I plan to have lots more.'

10

FALLING *STAR!*

A computer, had it been consulted, couldn't have put together a Hollywood movie more certain to become a hit. The star was the most beloved in the world. The director and producer had merely made the most successful film in history. The budget of $12 million was generous for 1968, and there was expensive location shooting in the south of France, Cape Cod, London, and New York. The songs were by George and Ira Gershwin, Kurt Weill, Noel Coward, and Irving Berlin. As befitted its glamorous subject, the jewels were from Cartier and the clothes were by Donald Brooks.

Yet *Star!*, which was about Gertrude Lawrence, starring Julie Andrews, directed by Robert Wise, produced by Saul Chaplin, and financed by Twentieth Century-Fox, who had been solvent again for three years running thanks to *The Sound of Music*, was the most complete disaster in the history of movie-making until Michael Cimino's *Heaven's Gate* in 1981. Richard Zanuck, then head of production at Fox, termed *Star!* 'my Edsel'. 'Jesus, but it was embarrassing,' said another Fox executive after the highly ballyhooed picture suffered a disastrous re-release under the title of *Those Were the Happy Times*.

Ironically, making the movie was a series of happy times for all concerned, and no one involved foresaw even a hint of the total artistic, critical, and commercial failure that *Star!* was to become. Wise had spent most of the three years since *The Sound of Music* preparing the picture, and Julie Andrews looked back on the year of her life spent as Gertrude Lawrence as 'the most stimulating thing I've ever done – and the most exhausting – though it put me off rhinestones forever'. For Julie, the biggest British musical comedy star since Gertrude Lawrence, the musical film was a fascinating study, leading to a generally sympathetic understanding of a woman she never knew or had even seen perform. The *Star!* experience revealed often eerie parallels in the lives of Andrews and Lawrence – even 'one or two rather unpleasant things about myself that I'd rather not think about'.

Julie was not yet seventeen when Lawrence died in 1952, shortly after her triumph in *The King and I* on Broadway. And *Star!* only took Lawrence's life story up to 1941, when Julie was only six. 'I'd heard some scratchy old records of hers a few times, but that was about it,' said Julie. Yet she was the first and only choice to play 'Gertie' from her vaudeville début at sixteen, through 95 per cent of all the scenes in the movie (several child actresses portrayed the stage star from ages six to fourteen, the first 5 per cent of the film, which was all done in black and white, documentary-style).

Robert Wise had decided to make another film with Julie Andrews even before they started *The Sound of Music*, and he was smart enough to sign her up for an unnamed second film at the same price, a comparatively meagre $225,000 with no percentage of the profits. 'I had someone spend six months digging into the Lawrence legend to see what was possible,' Wise recalled. 'Then I took it to Julie. I wouldn't have made the picture without her; if she hadn't wanted to do it, I'd have been busy on something else. The great drive was not to do the Gertrude Lawrence story, and we were interested in it only as a starring vehicle for Julie. She was always in it.'

Noel Coward was an important part of the Lawrence story, and it wouldn't be possible to do the film without his co-operation. Wise had already been turned down by Beatrice Lillie, who therefore was not portrayed at all in *Star!* despite her importance in her fellow performer's life. Wise recalled his nervous meeting with Coward in London. 'If he didn't agree, I knew we'd have to give up the whole idea. But the first thing he said was, "Who's going to portray me?" Daniel Massey was actually his choice, too. We'd been considering him on a list that included Robert Stephens and Peter Cook.'

With Coward's promise of co-operation Wise first mentioned the project to Julie during a luncheon lull during the filming of *The Sound of Music*, made longer by a spell of Alpine rain. As he sketched in the basic details of Lawrence's life, Julie said, 'That sounds a lot like me . . .' Before the rain stopped, she had agreed to the project as her second picture under her contract with Wise.

'Their lives are somewhat similar,' the director explained. 'Gertie was a product of music halls, a broken home, and step-parents, too. Physically there's a certain resemblance, although Julie's a far better singer than Gertie ever was. She was the proper age; we were taking Gertie from a young girl into her forties, and Julie can go either way. Both Julie and Gertie had great senses of humour. Gertie was a great clown and had a great love of gagging – Julie does too.'

'He fired my imagination by saying he didn't want to do the usual, glamorous backstage sort of story,' Julie said. 'Somehow the way he spoke about the theatre, how he wanted the draperies to be green velvet, and how he wanted to use old-fashioned theatres that Gertie used to play in, got me very excited.'

In the two months of pre-production on *Star!*, February and March 1967, Julie was fitted for ninety-four separate costumes that she would wear in the film. With *The Boy Friend* and *Thoroughly Modern Millie* in her past, Julie was no stranger to the fashions of the 1920s that would predominate in the first half of the film. But she was eagerly looking forward to her first fling into the 1930s. Studio tests led to thirty-six different sets of make-up for Julie's character and twenty different wigs, each of which could be reset significantly at least once. With these aids, during actual shooting, Julie could be forty first thing in the morning, twenty-two at lunchtime, and sixteen at sunset, and one day she actually was those three ages in that sequence. To accommodate the wigs (which would also be important to her next movie, *Darling Lili*), Julie cut her short hair even shorter and let it go from her lightened blonde back to her natural brown.

In pre-production Julie also rehearsed dances with choreographer Michael Kidd since she was to appear in twenty-one of the film's twenty-four musical numbers. Despite her days in vaudeville, Julie was the first to admit, 'I don't really dance; if they give me lots of fancy movements, I can make it *look* like I'm dancing.' She also pre-recorded six of the fifteen songs on which she soloed, including 'My Ship', 'Jenny', 'Someone To Watch Over Me', and 'Someday I'll Find You.'

When actual filming began in mid April Julie began to wear the largest single wardrobe ever fitted onto an actress in one work. Out of a schedule of 149 shooting days, Julie was on camera on all but seventeen (mostly when Wise and his crew were in London filming childhood scenes with the six juvenile actresses). Of 1,400 separate camera set-ups, Julie appeared in 1,372. Wise defended this excessive use of his star by saying, 'When a biographical story is being told in film, it is best to have the character be up on the screen nearly all the time rather than having other characters talk about her.' Richard Crenna, who played Lawrence's husband Richard Aldrich, put it another way: 'The rest of us are window-

In the Lyceum Theatre, New York, for the song 'Someone to Watch Over Me' from *Star!* 1968 TWENTIETH CENTURY-FOX

dressing.'

The film set another record – for the most sets ever assembled for one movie, 185 in all. There were twenty filming sites in London, fourteen different locations in New York, and historically important visits to the Cape Cod Playhouse in Dennis, Massachusetts, and to the south of France for several scenes at a private, $2-million, sea-coast villa called Medi Roc (where Lawrence attempted unsuccessfully to effect a reconciliation with her daughter, whom she had neglected in favour of her career).

For one week at the Lyceum Theatre in New York, the cast, abetted by nine hundred extras, simulated the 1926 opening of Gertrude Lawrence in the Gershwin's *Oh, Kay!* Julie sang 'Someone To Watch Over Me'. It had been six years since she sung on a Broadway stage, and Julie felt 'tingling all over, and suddenly realizing that I'm having the best of both worlds in one movie'.

Richard Aldrich, who had been producer at the Cape Cod Playhouse in 1939 when Lawrence worked there, and married her the next year, watched Crenna and Andrews recreate scenes of his life at the famous theatre, which was built in 1790. He saw the scene of his first encounter with Lawrence inside the Playhouse, she playing the temperamental big star, and he the cool, unimpressed small-town businessman. Aldrich also watched the actors run through a rain of rice, after the wedding, to a waiting Rolls-Royce. While he would make no public comment on Julie's portrayal of Gertie or Crenna's of himself, as he watched the scene in the Playhouse he was heard to whisper, almost to himself, 'Remarkable, how much . . .'

'When I got into the role,' said Julie, 'I couldn't wait to get my hands on all the things she had done. She was an incredibly multi-talented lady. Our voices are different, but I suggested her inflections and cadences here and there. But the routine was unbelievably rigorous; it was like going into training. I got up at 5.45 every day and had to be on the set by 7.00 a.m., and sometimes I didn't get home until 8.00 in the evening.'

Even on rehearsal days Julie had to go into the studio at 9.00 and stay until 6.00, and since she was in virtually every frame of the movie there were three separate shut-downs of filming to rehearse song and dance numbers. Her lunch hours were taken up with costume fittings, interviews, out-of-town visitors, and her agents and other business associates. On rare occasions Emma Kate came to the set of *Star!* for a visit. Every working day a doctor arrived to give Julie a vitamin shot. And at the end of every work day Blake Edwards would arrive to take her home.

'I can't converse on anything outside this movie,' she said in the middle of filming. 'I just manage to read the morning paper every day; when I go home at night I collapse. The pace of this film is unrelenting and merciless.'

There was, however, the time in the movie to think about Gertrude Lawrence. 'I found myself reflecting on her a lot,' Julie said. 'And I realized that in many ways she was a sad and lonely woman. Sometimes I'd get muddled – where did Gertrude leave off and where did I begin?'

To help her sort out the difference, Julie kept a file on her desk labelled *Impressions of Gertrude Lawrence – Confidential*. Julie's research showed that Lawrence was 'definitely a kook, eccentric, glamorous, and witty. There were the obvious biographical facts we had in common, like separated parents and starting in vaudeville' (to say nothing of a brief first marriage ending in divorce, one daughter, and a love affair with a producer).

Both actresses had played in the Welsh city of Swansea, and both achieved significant success playing Eliza Doolittle. (Julie didn't get to play Gertie playing Eliza because that production of *Pygmalion* was in 1945, and *Star!* ends with the opening of *Lady in the Dark* in 1941.) Moss Hart had directed Gertie in *Lady in the Dark*, and directed Julie in *My Fair Lady* fifteen years later.

Julie discovered several traits she and Lawrence had in

common. 'We both whistled a lot and we both were always lapsing into bits of cockney. She had a habit of singing a high note to relieve the tension. I do the same thing, sing as loud and as high as I can. She was extravagant. I am too – even more so after I played her. She would fill her dressing room with flowers; she once bought a large cherry tree because it was in bloom. I'm certainly not as extravagant of gesture, but I think I understand her quite well and I know how she felt. When you're in the theatre on matinée day, from noon until midnight, you don't see daylight. You want some living things in your room.'

The 'hateful' things that Julie found she and Gertie had in common were 'an absolute fear of any kind of commitment' and 'always putting on an act. She would play at being a mother one minute, a gardener the next, a shopper the next. I'm rather like that. I'm not as fiery a temperament as she was. She was not a terribly nice person; in fact, she was a real bitch at times.'

For that reason perhaps, and because up to that point in her career she had portrayed fictional heroines (with the one exception of the semi-fictional and highly romanticized Maria von Trapp), Julie said 'this feels like the first *character* I've ever done. But walking the fine line between caricature and tribute, and avoiding impersonations is not easy.'

Robert Wise was troubled during the production of *Star!* by Julie's failure to exploit the more flamboyant aspects of Lawrence's personality in her portrayal. 'If Julie has anything, it is a quality of honesty and truthfulness. And that has made her doubtful and given her difficulty with some of the theatricalities of Gertie's behaviour. If she has had to work hard on anything, it has been on the volatile and hammy aspects of Gertie. She doesn't quite realize yet how many things she can make her own.'

'This is not an attempt at a totally truthful portrait of Gertrude Lawrence,' Julie said, 'and I didn't feel I was *doing* anything like her. I certainly was not trying to sing like her; I

166

Singing 'Do, Do, Do' in *Star!* 1968 TWENTIETH CENTURY-FOX

don't think her voice was particularly strong or pretty. When you try to be someone, the temptation is to lay it on with mannerisms and speech. But if I did that, I'd only be applying it rather than feeling it myself. So the result was part me, part script, and part her. It was pleasant to play somebody real for once, but I was not trying to be faithful to the way people remember her – I don't think I could be.'

The London (and world) première of *Star!* at the Dominion Theatre had been originally scheduled for 4 July 1968, which would have been Gertrude Lawrence's sixty-seventh birthday. But it had been postponed until 11 September, then pushed back to 18 July, in both cases to accommodate the Duke and Duchess of Kent, who were the Royal patrons of the première, for the benefit of the National Advertising Benevolent Society. When the night came, Saul Chaplin and Robert Wise and their wives, both Darryl and Richard Zanuck, Richard Crenna and his wife, and others involved with the picture appeared. So did Noel Coward, Dame Edith Evans, Lord Louis Mountbatten, Cathleen Nesbitt, and Julie's mother, her father and stepmother, and two brothers.

Noel Coward had a pre-première cocktail party at his river suite in the Savoy Hotel, for some friends who remembered Gertrude Lawrence. Among them were Nesbitt and Anna Massey, whose father, Raymond, had played Higgins in *Pygmalion* opposite Lawrence, and whose brother Daniel played Coward in the film. Although he had contributed heavily to the screenplay, writing his own dialogue for Daniel Massey – without screen credit but with a sizeable stipend – Coward was sceptical about the final result.

As his group was leaving the Savoy for the Dominion, he said, 'It will unquestionably be a marvellous commercial film, and Julie and Danny will be marvellous. So will all those nostalgic, unforgettable songs. But it won't bear the slightest possible resemblance to the Gertie we knew.'

Thus *Star!* arrived – but its star didn't. The aeroplane that had been chartered to stand by at Heathrow Airport to fetch

The finale number, 'Jennie', in *Star!* 1968 TWENTIETH CENTURY-FOX

Julie from the Brussels location of *Darling Lili* had never left London. The flower-packed suite booked for her at the Dorchester Hotel would not be used. At the last minute, word came from Brussels that night-shooting on *Darling Lili* involving thousands of extras would keep Julie there. The Zanucks were furious and blamed Blake, Paramount Pictures, and professional jealousy. Crowds, both inside and outside the theatre, did not get the word immediately and disbelievingly, in vain, searched for the star. They were shattered when she did not show up. Even the Duchess of Kent asked, 'Where's Julie?'

Without Julie, *Star!* was shown to the public for the first time, and the première audience came down firmly on two sides: those who remembered Gertrude Lawrence on stage resented the portrait of her as written and played; those who didn't remember her were as charmed by *Star!* as by any other Julie Andrews musical.

The London critics divided approximately the same way, although they were harsher on the film for taking liberties with a recent life. When the film opened in New York in the fall of 1968, the critics were nothing short of scathing. (Julie also skipped that première, pleading pressing scenes on *Darling Lili*). WCBS TV's Leonard Harris, speaking for the majority, said, '*Star!* is a sort of gentile *Funny Girl*, and not nearly as good. It is a clichéd cataloguing of the life and hard times of Gertrude Lawrence . . . and it compounds its spurious attitudes towards show business with its terrible handling of the actual performance numbers.'

Star! was not the horror most critics made it out to be, but, although intermittently entertaining, it was less than very good. Audiences, for whatever reason, stayed away from the road-show release in America, although the film was a modest success in its first weeks in London. Twentieth Century-Fox withdrew the picture and re-released it after some cutting as a regular feature at regular prices. Still, even the hard-core Andrews fans didn't go to see it, and it was recalled all

170

together on 1 July 1969. Further cuts were made by the studio, bringing the film down to two hours, without consulting Robert Wise. The title was changed to *Gertie Was a Lady*, then to *Those Were the Happy Times*. But in re-release, the movie lasted only a week.

Every bit as inexplicably as *The Sound of Music* had become such a phenomenal success and confirmed Julie's position as box office queen of Hollywood, *Star!* did the opposite. The press and the public, both of whom had adored her for years, suddenly seemed to turn against her. And the turning point, if there was just one, had to be the world première of *Star!* in London when Julie failed to appear.

'Of all the premières,' she said, 'this was the one I really wanted to go to. This was home, one's family, royalty and all one's chums. I'd had a dress designed in Dublin, and of all the movies I made, this was the one I cared about most. But they changed the date twice – it was in my contract with Paramount that I would have the night of 4th July off no matter what – and we were in Belgium, behind schedule and with hundreds of extras involved. Up until three hours before the première I thought I was going to make it. Blake had figured out how to use a double for me in a long shot. But as the time got closer, we realized that even with that long shot – which he didn't really want to do – and having the cast and crew wait another hour or so, I could still only fly to London just in time to get to the theatre, walk through the front door, and walk right out again. I wouldn't even have got to see my family or friends. So I didn't go.'

Both Julie and Blake were embittered by the reaction of the British and American press to her non-attendance. He was even madder because Twentieth Century-Fox executives had called their counterparts in Paramount in Hollywood and begged them to call Blake in Brussels to get him to let Julie have the night off.

'How could anyone doubt that she wanted to go to the opening and that I wanted her to go?' Blake asked. 'It would

171

have been good for Paramount and for us too. But it was just impossible.'

Both studios, in turn, were angry with Edwards for what they considered an evil influence and final authority over his lady-friend and star. Paramount was particularly upset since he was spending their money hand over fist, and was millions over the budget of *Darling Lili* anyway. What was one night – even with nine hundred extras – more or less? No one at either studio doubted that Gertrude Lawrence, faced with the same situation, would have told her producer-director (even if he had been her lover) to go to hell and flown to London for at least two days.

11

THE $24-MILLION VALENTINE

DARLING LILI, was Blake's 'play with music', using, as *Star!*
had, existing songs of the period – in this case the First World
War. Henry Mancini and Johnny Mercer, who had written the
Academy Award winning songs 'Moon River' for Edwards'
Breakfast At Tiffany's, and 'Days of Wine and Roses' for the
director's film of the same name, wrote seven new songs for
Darling Lili, six of them for Julie. These included 'Whistling
Away the Dark', 'I'll Give You Three Guesses', 'Smile Away
Each Rainy Day' and 'A Girl In No Man's Land'.

Julie, in her role as British singing idol Lili Smith and
German spy Lili Schmidt, also sang 'Keep the Home Fires
Burning', 'It's a Long Way to Tipperary', and the French
national anthem, 'La Marseillaise'. The chief target of her
espionage was a handsome American dawn-patrol air squad-
ron commander who knew all the crucial Allied aerial and
troop manoeuvres, a part played by Rock Hudson.

In the film Lili tries to extract secrets from the commander
by seducing him, but she ends up falling in love with him.

Julie was changing her image even further in *Lili* by doing a comic strip-tease in a theatre in which she was only supposed to sing (the strip is done in a jealous fit to make the Hudson character mad); a little wrestling match with Hudson in bed; and a shower scene in which she is bare to the cleavage and he is fully clothed.

'I'm trying to be very still in this one,' said Julie. 'Lili isn't a lady who is bouncy. She's somebody who's cool and in perfect control, and then gets all gibberish.'

'We're playing this for realism,' said Blake. 'The sets, the action, the people are all as honest as we can make them. Julie plays an English lady who is loved by England and turns out to be a German spy. The humour in it arises out of characters. For example, Lance Percival is a cowardly Englishman who can only fly if he drinks, and he likes to drink, so he flies. He crashes and destroys six planes. There's absolutely nothing inconceivable about his character.'

The flying scenes alone guaranteed a big budget for *Darling Lili*, as did location shooting in Ireland, Belgium, and France. And Julie's salary for the picture was $1,100,000 against ten per cent of the gross receipts, a new Hollywood record. Blake, as producer, director, and co-author of the screenplay, was also well compensated. But the way *Darling Lili* began to go over budget, and cost its studio millions more than had been projected, contributed to the death of movie musicals, the old studio system, and the career of Julie Andrews.

Filming began pleasantly enough on the Paramount lot in March 1968. It was a congenial set, partly because Blake had his hand-picked associates around him. His father was serving as studio production manager, and his uncle was executive producer of the movie. Julie was brand-new to Paramount, and despite the flap over the *Star!* première, there was great excitement at having her on the lot. *Darling Lili* was the object of a great deal of curiosity, but the interior scenes in the early days of shooting posed no particular problems.

The day they shot the shower scene, the director, the star,

and her co-star were having a great time, and so was the crew. The scene had been shot three times, and Blake was satisfied with the third take, when Julie, soaking wet, asked, 'Darling, would you like to do another take?'

'Would you?'

'Not if you're happy.'

'You know what you need is to find a fellow, settle down, and marry him.'

''ood 'ave me?' (Lapsing into Eliza-like cockney)

'Some damn fool director.'

They kissed, and she reached to put her arms around him. 'Oh, no, you don't,' he said. 'You're all wet.'

Blake said, more seriously, 'I'd marry her tomorrow, but she can't marry me right now – her divorce isn't final. We're together, that's the important thing. Of course, if I do marry the leading lady I'll get 10 per cent of the profits of the picture,' he joked.

Up until the *Darling Lili* company went to its Dublin location, Julie and Blake continued to live in their separate houses. But they decided to move in together at Carton, a castle outside the Irish capital that doubled as a movie set in several sequences. It was elegant, private, wooded, and peaceful. Julie said she had never been happier any place. Carton was large enough to have four gate houses, several cottages, and unlimited livestock. When Rock Hudson hurt his foot, Julie was able to play Lady Bountiful and come down from the big house with a basket of goodies and a solicitous concern for his health. She went for long walks in the summer rain along a secluded garden path. The whole atmosphere seemed so right that she and Blake rented the castle again the next summer – just for a vacation.

They had finally agreed to live together openly because, in Blake's words, 'It seemed dumb not to admit we were in love.' Julie, typically less sure of herself in the situation, 'kept telling him it wasn't going to work,' she remembered.

The Irish weather was extremely uncooperative on the

picture. When a grey day was called for in the script, it was endless brilliant sunshine. There were several night scenes, and night in summer in Ireland began at 11.00 p.m. and lasted only until about 3.30 a.m. The Irish crews were not used to big Hollywood productions, and their uncertain work slowed things down considerably. When the company went on to Brussels there were more weather problems, more night shooting, and the added obstacle of bureaucratic inefficiency when it came to granting official permission for the use of buildings – a problem that was to be even worse in Paris.

'Everything that could have gone wrong went wrong,' Julie recalled. Filming was costing upwards of $70,000 a day, and because of the variable weather, scenes weren't matching properly and had to be re-shot. One cloudy day outside Paris, when sunshine was needed, Blake was trying to match outdoor close-ups of Andrews and Hudson with footage that had been shot in Ireland. At this point *Darling Lili* was five weeks behind schedule and an estimated $2 million beyond budget. Although he wanted to re-shoot several scenes in Europe, Paramount summoned Blake and his company back to Hollywood.

Even back at the studio, the production was troubled. With each rumour from the set, Julie's press worsened. One day the Paramount publicity department found itself with more stars making movies on the lot than at any time in more than a decade. Barbra Streisand was shooting *On a Clear Day You Can See Forever*, John Wayne was making *True Grit*, Lee Marvin and Clint Eastwood were finishing *Paint Your Wagon*, and Julie and Rock Hudson were there for *Darling Lili*. The studio decided to get them all together one afternoon for the kind of star group picture that hadn't been taken in a long time.

The actors, uncommonly, were all close to on time – except for Julie, who didn't show at all. The other stars, including Hudson, waited, and John Wayne said to Robert Evans, Paramount's head of production, 'Are you going to furnish

With Rock Hudson in *Darling Lili* 1970 PARAMOUNT PICTURES

chairs while we wait for the queen?' Evans himself went to the *Darling Lili* set and found her in a difficult crying scene that she had to do over and over again. Edwards told Evans he would not interrupt shooting for a publicity photograph, which Evans was forced to tell the other stars, who posed without her. The next morning Julie went to the dressing rooms of Barbra Streisand and some of the others, to apologize for holding them up in vain.

Edwards' self-indulgence or perfectionism, depending on one's viewpoint, left Paramount with '$15 million of unusable film and no picture', in the words of one top studio-production executive. There were individual scenes that were interesting, conceded some of the few Paramount officials who had seen the rushes, but they didn't add up to a saleable film of any sort, much less a big Julie Andrews road show, which is what *Darling Lili* would have to be if there were any chance of recouping the investment. The opening of the film was postponed to the spring of 1970 in the hope that it could be salvaged. In the meantime, the movie was costing even more money in interest on the capital invested in it, and taxes on unreleased film. The total cost of *Darling Lili*, therefore, was close to $24 million.

Blake's excesses and Julie's seemingly callous superstar behaviour quickly caused the press, even in her native England, to attack them with all knives bared. Even *Life* magazine, which loved movies and movie stars more than any other mass circulation periodical, refused to run a take-out on Julie written by their Hollywood correspondent because 'it wasn't bitchy enough.' Joyce Haber, a syndicated columnist whose home paper was the *Los Angeles Times*, ran a series of 'blind' items about celebrities, usually involving their sexual exploits. The personalities were identified by nicknames or initials only. In the case of Julie, Blake, and Rock Hudson, Haber had used the not very subtle appellations of Miss P and P (Prim and Proper); Mr X, the director of a major musical, now being filmed, who is conducting an affair with its leading lady, Miss P and P; and Mr VV (Visually Virile).

Haber contended that Julie and Blake had been making fun of Hudson for his allegedly less-than-manly behaviour on the set. The columnist reported that Blake had said, 'I don't understand people like that,' and that Julie had said to Rock, 'Remember, *I'm* the leading lady.' Haber also claimed that Mr VV had gone for a weekend to San Francisco and visited one of his favourite leather bars, only to walk in the door and

178

find Mr X leaning against the bar.

Julie and Blake both said that he could not have been in San Francisco at the time that Haber contended in her item. 'But suing her would have dignified her,' said Julie, who had been the victim of previous attacks by Haber and would be the subject of many more. Julie's only revenge came in her widely quoted remark: 'They should give Haber open-heart surgery and go in through the feet.' Blake's revenge came twelve years later in his movie *S.O.B.*, which had been inspired by his and Julie's negative experiences in Hollywood after *Darling Lili*. Loretta Swit played the gossip columnist based on Haber, who by then had long since been fired by the *Los Angeles Times*.

The last straw, even for the few remaining pro-Andrew members of the American press, came in February of 1969. The occasion was Alan Jay Lerner's twenty-fifth anniversary as a librettist and lyricist, and a testimonial dinner for the benefit for the American Academy of Dramatic Arts. All the stars who had sung his songs and many who had not were providing the evening's entertainment. Julie was one of four co-chairman, along with Rex Harrison, Richard Burton, and Barbra Streisand, who was then making the movie version of Lerner's *On a Clear Day You Can See Forever*. Burton was busy on a film in Europe and Streisand was excused with Lerner's permission and urging because she was needed in Hollywood for *On a Clear Day*. That left Julie and Rex Harrison, doing songs from *My Fair Lady*, as the highlights of the evening.

The affair was held on a Sunday evening at New York's Waldorf Astoria Hotel, and most out-of-town guests flew in the Friday before, in time for rehearsals. That Friday evening Julie called Alan Lerner from California at about the time she was due to arrive in New York. She said that she was terribly sorry, but she had a spot on her throat and the doctor had told her she shouldn't go to New York; besides, Blake was sick with bronchial pneumonia and she had to stay at home and take care of him. Lerner, of course, was the one person who couldn't plead with her to relent, or tell her to come off it, so he said he understood. Mrs Lerner, however, didn't understand, and she tried everything she could think of to get Julie to honour her commitment – even calling André Previn, Lerner's collaborator on *Coco*, to get him to call Julie.

Despite the worst snowstorm of the season, which had begun to fall at midnight on Saturday, by Sunday evening an estimated two-thirds of the 2,500 ticket-buyers somehow appeared at the benefit. Many had walked in high boots down a deserted Park Avenue through deep drifts of snow. Harrison did 'I've Grown Accustomed To Her Face', but the familiar face wasn't there. 'I Could Have Danced All Night' was quietly dropped from the programme and the only reference to Julie was made by the Master of Ceremonies, cartoonist Al Capp, who read congratulatory telegrams. Capp said, 'The one we love the most was from the universally beloved Julie Andrews, which says, "I can't make it." It is signed by her doctor, Sam Shepard, and I believe him and I believe her.'

Haber devoted a full syndicated column to Julie's no-show at the Lerner tribute in New York. 'Poor Julie will soon run out of excuses,' wrote the columnist, 'and what will her fans, her public defenders, say then? (I assure you, she has few important defenders in the industry.)'

While Blake tried to salvage *Darling Lili* in the cutting room, Julie went back to work in television. Although she had had a commercial and critical success with *The Julie Andrews Show*, a special she had done in 1965, once she had the choice, TV was her least favourite medium. The 1965 special, her first for NBC after several projects at CBS, had drawn thirty-five million viewers (more than Streisand or Sinatra that season), won two Emmys and a Peabody Award, and been successfully repeated in 1968.

Despite her feeling that television involved too many compromises in too little time, in November 1969 Julie taped

An Evening with Julie Andrews and Harry Belafonte
1969 NBC TELEVISION

a second special for NBC. *An Evening with Julie Andrews and Harry Belafonte* was directed, at her request, by Gower Champion, and had Michel Legrand as musical director. She agreed to do the show essentially because Hathaway House, the home for disturbed boys on the old De Mille estate in Hollywood that was her chief charity at the time, was offered the chance to produce the show and earn a percentage of the profits.

The special was staged with just the two performers on camera, singing virtually every song together or to each other, sometimes romantically, as they did for 'Scarborough Fair'. Champion explained the format by saying, 'The really memorable TV specials had been twos: Merman and Martin, Julie and Carol . . .' Belafonte was allowed one calypso number, and Julie had a fast finale medley of *My Fair Lady* and *Mary Poppins*. The pairing was something of a break-through for TV in terms of race relations. Belafonte, in an appearance on a Petula Clark special the previous year, had been the focal point of a major *scandale* when Petula merely touched his arm. This time, he said, 'I had no self-consciousness about how we'd relate and I was convinced that Julie had no hangups either. There was no network censor-ship, and Gower never pulled back because of colour. We cavort around the stage holding hands, dance and sing cheek to cheek – she's biting and kicking me all through the show. It could have been Frank Sinatra or Robert Goulet instead of me, or Lena Horne instead of her.'

Julie, who picked most of the songs for the special after several weeks' close attention to the pop stations on the radio in her new white Mercedes, succumbed to the finale medley after watching a Lena Horne special and finding herself 'never so happy as when she finally settled down to sing "Stormy Weather". If I reacted that way to her, I thought maybe some people would feel cheated if I didn't sing some-thing of the past.'

She still found working in television 'rushed and different',

With Rock Hudson on the set of *Darling Lili*
1968 PARAMOUNT PICTURES

despite a self-imposed ten-week rehearsal schedule, a huge
budget, and no audiences for either rehearsals or the final
taping. When Julie encountered Carol Burnett in a corridor at
NBC, where Carol was also taping, she said 'How do you do it
every week? You must have a marvellous nanny.'

A friend once described Julie as a lady of standards where
men were concerned: 'She's either dating or she's married.'

The situation with Blake didn't fit either category and it began to make her uncomfortable. Then his son Geoffrey came to live with Blake and Julie at her house in Beverly Hills; daughter Jenny soon followed, since she and Julie had developed a particularly strong relationship during the summer in Europe on *Darling Lili*. 'We could tell the kids were worried about our living together,' Blake recalled. 'To them marriage seemed important.'

'So I finally decided what the hell,' said Julie. 'It was just a piece of paper, and anyway it felt right.'

The wedding, on 12 November 1969, was held in secret at their house, at one o'clock in the afternoon, 'In the garden by the waterfall,' Blake said, 'because it's Julie's favourite place.' They bought wedding rings and got blood-tests from the family doctor the day before and left the house at eight in the morning on the day of the wedding to get a licence outside Los Angeles county (so the press wouldn't find out). Julie informed the staff only that morning, and the children only when they came home from school at noon. 'Otherwise they'd have wanted to take the day off from school,' Blake explained. Blake and Julie got married, then attended the first screening of *Darling Lili* at Paramount later that afternoon.

A legal family at last, the Edwards bought a bigger house in Beverly Hills and built a beach house in Malibu. Under the circumstances, they were pleased with *Darling Lili*, and Paramount's decision to go ahead and release it as a road show in New York and Los Angeles in the spring of 1970. Both Julie and Blake seemed to have held on to their professional possibilities, and Jennifer Edwards had made a creditable acting début as Heidi in a television version of the classic story.

'From the moment we got married a new quality was added,' said Blake, 'and we said to each other, "There's a kind of commitment we've just made that I don't think we made before." Early on we had certain realities to face. Although Julie's career was important to her, we also had a large family. That's not to say chauvinistically that a woman's place is in the home. But I might survive without the family. I couldn't survive without my profession. I had a bit of trouble in the beginning; it was a kind of childish jealousy. We men endow our women with a bit of mother image, and when our woman turns her attention towards her career and the men in that career, whoever they are – agents, leading men whoever they are – a little bit of jealousy creeps up. We had a couple of good long talks about it, because Julie won't let me get away with talking rubbish. If she sees me becoming too childish, her favourite phrase is "Bullshit, Blackie!" In the face of that, what can you do?'

The problem was solved by the failure of *Darling Lili*. Although many critics liked the film, and it broke box office records in its initial release at Radio City Music Hall in New York, the film didn't do well in the rest of the country or overseas. Suddenly Julie Andrews was box office poison; the two failures in a row finished her movie career, and she was actually paid $1 million *not* to make the film version of the Broadway musical *She Loves Me*, a humiliation never suffered by another star before or since. MGM also dropped its plans to do Irving Berlin's *Say it with Music*, which Blake and Julie were to have done together.

'I was depressed by the failure of *Star!* and *Darling Lili*,' she said, 'and I regretted not going into another musical right away to make up for them. But musicals, big or small, just weren't being made then.

'It was really like coming out of a long tunnel – I'd done nothing but work for so long, and I felt great exhaustion. I'm usually very honest with myself, and I think I'd admit it now if I felt I was particularly difficult on the set of *Star!* and *Darling Lili*. I was very tired, and late a number of times, usually because they'd scheduled four or five costume fittings when I should have been eating breakfast or lunch. I decided I was damned well going to get something to eat, and to hell with what people thought. There are times when you have to be rather ruthless if you are trying to survive.'

The press, which had already turned against her, played its part in her fast professional demise, a fact which has made Julie timid about interviews ever since. 'There's an unwritten law in Hollywood that says once you're on a pedestal let's throw some rocks and knock her off it,' she felt. Blake termed the attacks on her 'vicious' and said they came about because she was 'a threat to a lot of ladies and some gentlemen, too, because she appears to be something they have made up'.

A changing Hollywood, having created Julie Andrews and apparently used her up, was now ready to throw her out. She wouldn't make another movie until 1974, and that on foreign locations, and for Blake Edwards, as part of her English television deal, and she wouldn't make another for five years after *that* – also for Blake, and this time in a supporting part. Their fourth film together, 1981's *S.O.B.* would tell some of the story of the post *Darling Lili* decline in both their careers.

In retrospect, it seemed that Hollywood didn't know what to do with Julie Andrews, her 'wholesome' image that she had tried so hard to change, and the director who had helped her to change it. 'At the time I didn't think about it,' she said. 'Trends change, and this year's hit is soon forgotten. How to keep up is the problem. There's a line in *S.O.B.* that says, "Every time I think I know where it's at, it's usually somewhere else." You can only try to do what pleases you. I just tried to pick nice roles.'

12

THE VANILLA MOMENTS

WHEN she couldn't get work, or at least not the kind she preferred (theatre, nightclubs and television were offered to her all the time), Julie found that her drive to succeed wasn't nearly so great as it had been for most of her life. 'When Blake and I first married,' she said, 'I needed to work less – for emotional reasons. I kept very busy with home and family, and was very happy. I found I didn't miss work. My daughter was able to become part of my life. I would never have believed that I'd be able to stop work the way I did. I agreed to do just enough to keep my ego reasonably high, mainly a follow-up television special with Carol Burnett. I attended a ballet class for a while, but I found it took up too much time. The days were terribly busy, although I couldn't tell you what I did except get involved with some charities. Finally I got down to essentials: Blake and the children.'

The special with Burnett, who by now had a regular weekly variety series of her own on television, was called *Julie and Carol at Lincoln Centre*, and in that New York emporium it followed the format of *Julie and Carol at Carnegie Hall*, and was taped one hot July night in 1971 straight through, with a live audience, for telecasting later that year. While it was not the critical smash of the original special nine years before, it was a pleasant, professional hour that had respectably large viewing figures. Julie may have been through in movies, but there was a home for her on the small screen if ever she wanted it.

Finally, in 1972, she did. Lew Grade went to Hollywood to sign the 'biggest single deal I have ever completed for ITV'. Julie was to do twenty-four shows for ATV in England and ABC in America for a number of years, plus one feature film per year, not necessarily a musical. Her participation in the profits would earn her a minimum of £2 million (then $5 million) for the first two years, with options to continue for another three years. Lord Lew said, 'I have dreamed of doing a TV series with Julie for years. I first met her when I was a theatrical agent and she came into my office, a little girl with a beautiful singing voice. All the American networks have been chasing Julie, but I persevered for three years and she said she had no excuses left and agreed to sign the contract.'

What convinced her to sign, of course, was the movie clause. She had never accepted the verdict of the public on *Star!* and *Darling Lili* as the final word on her movie career, and she had had three years to reflect on it. 'I pulled through,' she said, 'largely because I believed in those pictures and disagreed with the critical and popular estimate of them. *Star!* failed because the public wasn't very happy with seeing me in the drunken scenes, but I wanted to show that at times Gertie was almost silly, and they couldn't accept me as a spy in *Lili* and that disappointed me awfully.'

Julie stopped singing for the three years between the finish of *Darling Lili* and the start of *The Julie Andrews Hour* on television. 'There was no incentive to sing,' she said, 'It's a very lonely business, just you at the piano, practising, and very hard to do if you have no particular reason. The desire

With her Emmy Award 1973

just slipped away. I felt no great anxiety about it. Strange as it may sound, I have never found singing easy or enjoyable. I think I have a fear of finding it so, probably from having a little too much of it when I was young. In the back of my mind and the bottom of my heart I want to lick that.'

Getting back into shape for her show, 'There was a terrible moment when I found I was producing sounds, but I thought I'd forgotten to do it well. It takes about six weeks to put a voice into shape again, and at times I worried that it had really gone for good. But I think it was a sign of maturity to be able to stop singing for so long without worrying too much. When I was a small girl I wanted to be good, but I didn't believe in myself. Maturity took a long time.'

Thirty-seven years old when she began doing *The Julie Andrews Hour*, Julie said, 'Occasionally I feel a bit ridiculous tripping through the daffodils with eighteen young dancers in sneakers. I don't want to grow old, I don't know anybody who does. I'm not as young as I was, and in five more years I won't feel as young as I do now. I may not have the energy to do exhausting jitterbugs or tap dances.'

The series pushed the Mary Poppins image hard, and this time Julie seemed to go along with it. There was one recurring sketch in which Alice Ghostley played Julie's room-mate; Julie was organized, popular, unfailingly cheerful, and Alice was the opposite. Alice would look into the camera and say, 'Isn't she perfect? Don't you hate her?' Julie sang songs from her past successes, and took few chances with guest stars.

Robert Goulet, Steve Lawrence, Jack Cassidy and the real Maria von Trapp appeared. However, Julie could not get the other variety stars of the 1960s to come on her programme. Perry Como, Danny Kaye and Andy Williams were all announced as guest stars on *The Julie Andrews Hour,* but none of them showed up – in retaliation for Julie's failure to be a guest on their shows. (Como later did a special with Julie on *Sesame Street.*)

One unlikely guesting, by the late singer Cass Elliott,

190

proved a surprise – to Elliott. 'I was not prepared to like Julie,' she said, 'but she surprised me. One night we were working until four in the morning, and the actors were ready to kill each other. Julie was putting out on every take as if it were the last one she'd ever make. I was embarrassed to complain. There's something very special there that you grow to love. If she could just "free it up" a bit – groovy.'

There were a lot of late nights, and all early calls on the television series – although she was picked up each morning in a helicopter. 'A lot of the sacrifices I learned to take for granted,' she said, 'and didn't notice until I gave up work for a while. When I was doing the show Blake and I swapped roles completely. For the first two months I felt relieved that he was taking care of everything, but then I began feeling left out. He had to cook on the servants' day off. Blackie cooks like a dream – the best I can do is scrambled eggs and pot of tea – but he uses every pot and opens every cupboard. I clear up the mess so the effort evens up a little.'

The Julie Andrews Hour was a critical success, and won seven Emmys and a Silver medal at Montreux. But its ratings were abysmal, even after a time change, and the show was cancelled in its first year. 'That hurt for a long time,' she said. 'I found out we'd been cancelled at the same time the general public did. There was no personal message, no politeness about it.'

Just as Julie was failing in her television series, Blake's career as a Hollywood director seemed to be at a bitter end. He fought with MGM over his *Wild Rovers*, and quit the same studio's *The Carey Treatment* after the completion of principal photography. He was told, in effect if not literally, that he would never work in Hollywood again. Since it seemed that Julie wouldn't either, the couple and their family headed for Europe. For tax reasons they became residents of Switzerland, and settled in Gstaad, where they had vacationed so often, but they also acquired a house in London's Chester Square.

'My husband gave me a taste of American life,' Julie said on leaving her adopted country after ten years' permanent residence. 'Now it is up to me to show him what England has to offer.' This was in the summer of 1973.

England offered them both several television specials for Lew Grade, and one movie under the original contract, *The Tamarind Seed*, which Blake wrote and directed, and in which Julie starred with Omar Sharif. She played a secretary for the British Home Office and he played a military attaché for the Soviet Union. They meet in Barbados, where both are vacationing, causing their respective governments to worry about exchange of secrets. Julie's face is disfigured by a bomb in the somewhat downbeat Edwards screenplay, based on an Evelyn Anthony novel. Before that, there is a love scene between her and Sharif, directed by Blake. 'There I was in bed with another man,' she said, 'and my husband is telling me to do it better!'

The Tamarind Seed was shot mostly on location, in places like Barbados, Paris, London and Gstaad, which was supposed to be Canada. Sharif, Julie found, was 'very disciplined and great fun to work with; he is much loved on the set. I didn't discuss bridge with him, though, I would have been out of my depth.'

The movie, on release in 1974, did well overseas but died in the United States, causing a further setback in the careers of both Julie and Blake. He began complaining again about the Hollywood system that had deprived them both of their preferred livelihoods. 'But she wouldn't let me cop out,' he recalled, 'she just said, "Bullshit, Blackie, all you have to do is make another hit".'

He did just that, with Peter Sellers and *The Return of the Pink Panther*. But Julie again took a subordinate role. 'My life does now depend on what he is doing,' she explained, 'rather than doing my own thing as I used to.' She even took a cameo role as a maid in *The Return of the Pink Panther* so that they could be together. But her two-line part, which she played in a

With Omar Sharif in *The Tamarind Seed* 1974 JEWEL PRODUCTIONS LTD
and PIMLICO FILMS LTD

black wig and padding that made her unrecognizable, ended up on the cutting room floor. 'I've never been cut out of a picture,' she kidded, 'and now my own husband does it to me after I worked for free.'

Julie wrote two children's books in the early 1970s, *Mandy* and *The Last of the Really Great Whangdoodles*. The first was written for her stepdaughter Jenny, who extracted the story as a punishment for Julie's swearing; Julie had instituted a system of 'forfeits' for all the family for such misbehaviour as not brushing one's teeth. Written under her married name of Julie Edwards, *Mandy* was the story of an orphan girl who longs for a family, while *Whangdoodles* was written, Julie said, 'for the child in all of us'.

However, 'My husband is the real writer in the family,' she insisted, 'his work is the important stuff – but he is my best critic, and my toughest.'

Charity work still claimed some of Julie's time, and Hathaway House was a concern, even from a distance. She went back to Hollywood to be Mistress of Ceremonies at the dedication of a new 310-acre $3,900,000 – ranch facility for Hathaway House's disturbed children. The California Governor at the time, Ronald Reagan, also attended the dedication. Julie wore white gloves.

As the Vietnam War ended, she also became involved in the Committee of Responsibility, which brought war-injured Vietnamese children to America for medical treatment. This affiliation inspired her and Blake to adopt two orphaned Vietnamese girls, whom they named Amy Leigh and Joanna Lynn. 'We wanted a child and weren't being successful,' Julie recalled. 'While we were talking about adoption André Previn and Mia Farrow adopted a Vietnamese orphan girl. We took our son and daughter to the Previns' home to see their new daughter before any final decision was made. 'Emma took some persuading,' said Julie, 'but finally said, "All right, Mummy, as long as you don't ask me to babysit." Now she's the biggest mother to the babies of us all.'

Las Vegas 1976 POLLY HOWARD PHOTO

Both babies were flown from Saigon to Europe, and taken to Gstaad. They were sickly and fragile on arrival but blossomed into healthy toddlers in the Swiss mountain air. They were taken to America to be given American citizenship, but like the rest of the Edwards family in the late 1970s and early 1980s, considered Gstaad their real home. 'It's just a village, really,' said Julie, 'with duckies, piggies and horses. We have a dream house, with the most beautiful view in the world. The best time is being there. We can close the doors against the world, and hole up and hide. In Gstaad, I have always felt there is nothing that can harm me – ever.'

In 1976, Caesar's Palace in Las Vegas made Julie 'a tremendous offer I couldn't refuse; Blake talked me into going ahead.' The hotel offered Julie $250,000 a week for two shows a night. 'For what you're paying me I'll sell flowers in the casino,' she told the hotel's management. But it turned out to be an unhappy experience on both sides. She sold out two shows a night for a week, but did not draw the gambling crowds that Las Vegas needs to thrive. 'I just about burst a blood vessel every night trying to prove something to myself and I don't know why,' she said, 'I guess it's because if someone asked me, "What do you do?", I'd say, "I sing."' The remaining seven weeks of her eight-week contract were cancelled by mutual consent.

Returning to the London Palladium earlier that same year had been at the same time a happier and scarier experience. 'It isn't the teenage me in my size-eight Cinderella glass slipper,' she explained. 'It's me at forty, putting all my accumulated experience on the line.' The response in her home town encouraged Julie to take on a US-Japanese concert tour in 1977, eliminating other people's pop songs from her act, and going back to the standard numbers that she did best, like Jerome Kern's 'I'm Old-Fashioned'. 'I was taught good singing technique early,' she said. 'With my perfect enunciation I need a perfect lyric. A lot of the modern things are repetitive. I admire them, but I don't do them justice.'

196

With Dudley Moore and Bo Derek in *10* 1979 ORION PICTURES COMPANY

Her staple finale, whether in London, Las Vegas or Tokyo, was 'I Could Have Danced All Night', and her encore was always 'The Sound of Music'. These, together with 'Camelot', she termed, with no trace of sarcasm, 'the show's vanilla moments'.

Although back at work, Julie continued to refuse movie offers – turning down $500,000 to do *International Velvet* – mainly because 'I don't like what's going on. It's not sour grapes, it's the times. The four-letter words are flying, every other actress bares her bosom in one picture or another, the stories are becoming more and more trashy or totally far out and women have a worse and worse deal of it. I just want to make sure that if I do go back to the screen I don't make a fool of myself. I'm prepared to wait a few years until something right comes along.' She waited until Blake cast her in a secondary part in 1979's *10*. It proved to be the director's biggest commercial film, and coming on the heels of the Pink Panther revival re-established him in Hollywood, just as Julie had predicted it would. It did considerably less for her, overshadowed as she was by Dudley Moore and Bo Derek.

'Blake was always thinking of me as Sam,' she said, 'and although it's not a huge role I did it for him because I was involved with the script for so long – and it's such an important step in the development of Blake's work. But it was not a comeback for me, because I never retired.'

Dudley Moore, who became a romantic leading man in *10*, said of Julie, who played the girlfriend he leaves in pursuit of his ideal (Bo Derek): 'She's a very down-to-earth regular person. I don't think she's ever thought of herself as a huge celebrity, although God knows she is one. She has a huge following even now, but I think she has a need to be liked. We all do, but she's honest about it.'

Inexplicably, since Blake wasn't involved, Julie next took on the third re-make of *Little Miss Marker*, the movie that made Shirley Temple a star in 1934. Walter Matthau played Sorrowful Jones, the bookie, and Sara Stimson was cast in the

Julie gets ready to strip in *S.O.B.*, as William Holden, Loretta Swit, Robert Preston, Richard Mulligan and Stuart Margolin look on 1981 LORIMAR PRODUCTIONS, INC.

title part. 'The character Julie Andrews plays [a penniless heiress who lends her estate to a gambling operation] wasn't even in the original,' said Walter Bernstein, the screenwriter and director of the re-make. 'I wanted to take some of the emphasis off the child and put Matthau in a romantic situation. The role will show the good toughness and sexuality Julie had in *The Americanization of Emily*.'

It did nothing of the kind, since Julie looked as if she had shot much of the emotionless film with a migraine, but the movie was a disaster on release and was seen only on cable television in most areas. Yet during the making of *Little Miss Marker*, Julie charmed yet another leading man. Matthau said, 'She's a total delight, witty, bright and beautiful. She was exactly what I expected her to be – an excellent person with a great sense of humour. I can't understand the people who fall into the Mary Poppins trap. I never expected Julie to be any of the parts she's played, and of course she isn't.'

Julie's on-screen time amounted to about half an hour and the filming of it, for her, was not a happy experience. 'I've never played a seductress before. It's a terribly difficult role for me, and it shows.'

Julie's next two movies, both for Blake, were calculated to put Mary Poppins to rest forever, if such a thing were possible. *S.O.B.*, which Blake had been trying to get made for eleven years (finally making a deal only after the phenomenal success of *10*), stood for 'Standard Operating Bullshit'. 'It's a phrase Blake and I use all the time when something happens,' Julie explained. 'The film makes a strong statement about the way business is done in Hollywood and its standard operating bullshit. The minute anyone out there thinks you have something valuable, they are interested. But they couldn't care less if they don't think your project is going to make lots of money. It's a crazy business.'

In it, Julie plays a parody of herself, a movie actress best known for family musicals, surrounded by the leeches and loonies of tinseltown. 'All the characters are out of real life,' she said, 'any day you can see them out there. It all happened. Although it's done over the top in terms of comedy, it's mostly a true story.'

The character of Julie's husband in *S.O.B.* is a successful

From the MGM release *Victor/Victoria* © 1982
METRO-GOLDWYN-MAYER FILM CO.

writer-director whose current kiddie musical promises to be a box office disaster. To save it, the character (played by Richard Mulligan) turns the movie within the movie into a pornographic film. Thus, standing in front of a dozen mirrors, with most of *S.O.B.*'s crazy characters looking on (agent, gossip columnist, quack doctor who dispenses 'vitamin' shots, *et al.*), Julie removes the top half of her red gown and bares her firm 'boobies', as her character keeps calling them. The look on her face at that moment says, 'Everybody, take your image of me and stuff it.'

Julie's defence of the scene was curt: 'I'm an actress, and the part called for it. I've always had a rather nice body, but people who had only seen my movies assumed I was either sexless or puritanical.'

Unfortunately, nobody much cared one way or the other about Julie's bare breasts, and the parody of Hollywood in the late 1960s was almost fifteen years too late. (Blake had been trying to do the picture for at least eleven of those years, but as Julie put it, 'Every studio in Hollywood turned it down. Blake believed in it enough and finally someone took it. I believe the time factor was on our side – by waiting we made a better picture.') The general public could not involve itself in the problems and frustrations of very wealthy movie-makers, and *S.O.B.* failed at the box office – despite a Lear jet whistle-stop publicity campaign by Julie, Robert Preston, Mulligan and most of the picture's other stars.

In *Victor/Victoria*, which Blake had written for Julie and Peter Sellers (Preston replaced Sellers after his death), Julie played a woman pretending to be a man who works as a female impersonator in Paris in the 1930s. Henry Mancini and Leslie Bricusse wrote the songs Andrews and Preston sing in the nightclub sequences, making *Victor* another movie with music rather than a movie musical. Many of the film's extras were transvestites recruited from gay clubs around London.

At La Cage aux Folles nightclub in Los Angeles, imperson-

From the MGM release *Victor/Victoria* © *1982*
METRO-GOLDWYN-MAYER FILM CO.

ator Kelly Lawrence, like all other hardcore Andrews fans
around the world, was praying that *Victor/Victoria* would be a
hit. Kelly, who had been 'doing' Julie for seven years, found

that he had to drop from his act (which was 'lip-synched' to Julie's records) the later Andrews material – even the more sophisticated members of the Cage aux Folles audiences were indifferent to it – and go back to those 'vanilla moments' from *My Fair Lady* and *The Sound of Music*.

If *Victor/Victoria* is a success on its opening in April 1982, then Julie might continue in what has become the family business. Jennifer Edwards, twenty-six, is still pursuing her acting career (she played a small part in *S.O.B.*, as a hitch-hiker); Geoffrey, worked as an assistant editor on *10* and *S.O.B.* for his father; Emma Kate, nineteen, is studying ballet and considering a career in theatre. Even the only two children still at home full time, Amy and Joanna, eight and seven, have been introduced to their mother's other world. Julie took them to Disneyland, where 'we had an exhausting time doing about three days' worth of rides in one,' she recalled. (*Mary Poppins* remained Disney's top-grossing movie, and the division of Disney that manufactured the moving figures for Disneyland and Disney World was gratefully called MAPO in its honour – in the world of Disney, at least, Julie was still a superstar.)

Amy and Joanna had never seen their mother's movies, so they were shown, in late 1981, the musicals and *Hawaii*. 'Joanna fell asleep during *Sound of Music* and had to be taken off to bed,' Julie remembered. 'The next morning she was in tears. "I thought you said that was a happy movie." "It is in the end," I told her. "Well, I saw it," she said, "and it was terribly sad." They are just now starting to understand what it is that Mummy does for a living. Occasionally I take them to the studio with me for haircuts, but otherwise they don't have much contact with the business.'

Whether Julie would work again, she said, 'all depends on whether Blake is involved in the project or approves it, and whether it suits my schedule with the children. My principal occupation is being a wife to my director and a mother to our children. It is the most unlikely marriage, I still think we are a

With daughter Emma and Blake 1976

rather odd couple, yet it seems to work. We vowed we would take it a day at a time and never get a great fantasy about the way it was going to be in the future. But he is very good for me, he is straight and tells me when things are rubbish, and frequently pulls me up when I go straying into something that's wrong for me. Life is tremendous fun with him. I always wonder what he is going to come up with next. Just going out to dinner with him is a treat.'

After twelve years of her second marriage and her expanded family life, Julie's priorities were clear at last. While she would undoubtedly continue to make forays into the show-business world that had been with her literally her whole life, she said, 'I certainly wouldn't compare the rewards of watching one's children grow and mature with that of money piling up at the box office. Both are pleasant, but to varying degrees.

'As the old saying goes, you can't take the audience home with you. You can't depend on the loyalty of fans, who, after all is said and done, are just faceless people one seldom sees. And few stars have their fans forever. But a child is forever; that bond and relationship is timeless and doesn't depend on your looks, age or popularity at the moment.'

JULIE ANDREWS ON BROADWAY

1. *The Boy Friend*: 1954–5 season; produced by Cy Feuer and Ernest Martin; directed by Vida Hope; book, music and lyrics by Sandy Wilson; choreography by John Heawood; with John Hewer, Dilys Lay, Ruth Altman, Eric Berry, Ann Wakefield, Bob Scheerer, Geoffrey Hibbert.

2. *My Fair Lady*: 1956–8; 1958–9 London; produced by Herman Levin; directed by Moss Hart; book and lyrics by Alan Jay Lerner; music by Frederick Loewe; choreography by Hanya Holm; production designed by Oliver Smith; costumes by Cecil Beaton; with Rex Harrison, Stanley Holloway, Robert Coote, Cathleen Nesbitt, John Michael King, Phillipa Bevans.

3. *Camelot*: 1960–2; produced by Moss Hart, Alan Jay Lerner and Frederick Loewe; directed by Moss Hart; book and lyrics by Alan Jay Lerner; music by Frederick Loewe; choreography by Hanya Holm; production designed by Oliver Smith; costumes by Adrian and Tony Duquette; with Richard Burton, Roddy McDowall, Robert Goulet, Robert Coote and M'el Dowd.

THE FILMS OF
JULIE ANDREWS

1. *Mary Poppins*: released 1964; Buena Vista; Walt Disney,
producer; Robert Stevenson, director; music by Robert B.
and Richard M. Sherman; with Dick Van Dyke, Glynis Johns,
David Tomlinson, Hermione Baddeley, Ed Wynn, Matthew
Garber, Karen Dotrice, Elsa Lanchester, Jane Darwell.
(Oscars to Julie Andrews for Best Actress; the Shermans for
Best Original Score, Best Song ('Chim, Chim Cheree'); also
Best Editing and Best Visual Effects)
2. *The Americanization of Emily*: 1964; Metro-Goldwyn-
Mayer (Filmways); Martin Ransohoff, producer; Arthur
Hiller, director; screenplay by Paddy Chayefsky; music by
Johnny Mandel; with James Garner, Melvyn Douglas, Joyce
Grenfell, James Coburn, Keenan Wynn.
3. *The Sound of Music*: 1965; Twentieth Century-Fox;
Robert Wise, producer and director; screenplay by Ernest
Lehman; music by Richard Rodgers, lyrics by Oscar Ham-
merstein II (additional words and music by Richard Rod-
gers); with Christopher Plummer, Eleanor Parker, Peggy

Wood, Richard Haydn, Charmian Carr. (Oscars to Wise for Best Picture and Best Director; also Best Editing, Best Sound and Best Music Score: Adaptation)

4. *Hawaii*: 1966; United Artists (the Mirisch Company); Walter Mirisch, producer; George Roy Hill, director; Dalton Trumbo and Daniel Taradash, screenplay; music by Elmer Bernstein; with Max von Sydow, Richard Harris, Jocelyne La Garde.

5. *Torn Curtain*: 1966; Universal; Alfred Hitchock, producer and director; screenplay by Brian Moore; music by John Addison; with Paul Newman, Lila Kedrova.

6. *Thoroughly Modern Millie*: 1967; Universal; produced by Ross Hunter, directed by George Roy Hill; screenplay by Richard Morris; music score by Elmer Bernstein; musical numbers scored by André Previn; with Mary Tyler Moore, Carol Channing, James Fox, John Gavin, Beatrice Lillie. (Oscar to Elmer Bernstein for Best Music Score)

7. *Star!*: 1968; Twentieth Century-Fox; produced by Saul Chaplin; directed by Robert Wise; screenplay by William Fairchild; music arranged and conducted by Lennie Hayton; with Richard Crenna, Michael Craig, Daniel Massey, Bruce Forsyth, Beryl Reid, Garrett Lewis.

8. *Darling Lili*: 1970; Paramount; produced and directed by Blake Edwards; screenplay by Blake Edwards and William Peter Blatty; music score by Henri Mancini; new songs by Johnny Mercer and Henry Mancini; with Rock Hudson, Jeremy Kemp, Lance Percival, Michael Witney, Gloria Paul.

9. *The Tamarind Seed*: 1974; Avco-Embassy (ITC); Ken Wales, producer; Blake Edwards, director and screenplay; music by John Barry; with Omar Sharif, Anthony Quayle, Daniel O'Herlihy, Sylvia Sims, Oscar Homolka.

10. *10*: 1979; Warner Brothers (Orion); Blake Edwards and Tony Adams, producers; Blake Edwards, director and screenplay; music by Henry Mancini; with Dudley Moore, Bo Derek, Robert Webber, Dee Wallace, Sam Jones, Brian Dennehey, Max Showalter.

11. *Little Miss Marker*: 1980; Universal; Jennings Lang, producer; Walter Bernstein, director and screenplay; music by Henry Mancini; with Walter Matthau, Tony Curtis, Sara Stimson, Bob Newhart, Lee Grant.

12. *S.O.B.*: 1981; Paramount (Lorimar); Blake Edwards and Tony Adams, producers; Blake Edwards, director and screenplay; music by Henry Mancini; with William Holden, Robert Preston, Richard Mulligan, Shelley Winters, Marisa Berenson, Larry Hagman, Robert Loggia, Stuart Margolin, Craig Stevens, Loretta Swit, Robert Vaughn, Robert Webber, Jennifer Edwards.

13. *Victor/Victoria*: Metro-Goldwyn-Mayer; 1982; produced and directed by Blake Edwards; screenplay by Blake Edwards; music by Henry Mancini with James Garner, Robert Preston.

The Singing Princess, a 1967 cartoon, used the voice of Julie Andrews from early 1940s recordings.

JULIE ANDREWS DISCOGRAPHY (LPs only)

The Boy Friend: original Broadway cast, with John Hewer, Dilys Lay; composed and with lyrics by Sandy Wilson
RCA LOC–1018   1955
*My Fair Lady: original Broadway cast, with Rex Harrison, Stanley Holloway, Robert Coote; composed by Frederick Loewe, lyrics by Alan Jay Lerner
Columbia OL–5090   1956   Phillips RBL–1000   1957
*High Tor: original television cast, with Bing Crosby; composed by Arthur Schwartz, lyrics by Maxwell Anderson
Decca DL 8272   1956
Cinderella: original television cast, with Alice Ghostley, Kaye Ballard, Ilka Chase, Jon Cypher; composed by Richard Rodgers, lyrics by Oscar Hammerstein II
Columbia OL–5190   1957   OS–2005 *Stereo*
*The Lass with the Delicate Air
RCA LPM–1403   1957   LSP–1403 *Stereo*
*Julie Andrews Sings
RCA LPM–1681   1958   LSP–1681 *Stereo*
* No longer in catalogue.

Tell It Again: Rhymes with Martyn Green
Angel 65041   1958
Rose-Marie: with Giorgio Tozzi; music by Rudolf Friml and Herbert Stothart, lyrics by Otto Harbach and Oscar Hammerstein II
RCA LOP 1001 (RD–27143 in Great Britain)   1958
My Fair Lady: original London cast, with Rex Harrison, Stanley Holloway; composed by Frederick Loewe, lyrics by Alan Jay Lerner
Columbia OS–2015 *Stereo*   1959
Camelot: original Broadway cast, with Richard Burton, Robert Goulet, Roddy McDowall; composed by Frederick Loewe, lyrics by Alan Jay Lerner
Columbia OS–8521 *Stereo*   1961
CBS–7009   Also KOS–2031 (different cover)
Broadway's Fair Julie
Columbia CS–8521 *Stereo*   1962
Julie and Carol at Carnegie Hall: original television cast, with Carol Burnett; composed and with lyrics by Mike Nichols, Ken Welch and others
Columbia OS–2240 *Stereo*   1962
Don't Go into the Lion's Cage Tonight
Columbia CS–8686 *Stereo*   1962
Mary Poppins: original motion picture Sound-track, with Dick Van Dyke; composed and with lyrics by Richard M. and Robert B. Sherman
Buena Vista STER–5005 *Stereo*   1964
The Sound of Music: original motion picture Sound-track, with Christopher Plummer; composed by Richard Rodgers, lyrics by Oscar Hammerstein II
RCA LSOD–2005 *Stereo*   1965
A Christmas Treasure: with André Previn conducting
Firestone SLP–7012   1966   RCA LSP–3029   1967

* No longer in catalogue.

Thoroughly Modern Millie: original motion picture Sound-track, with James Fox, Carol Channing; title song by Sammy Cahn and James Van Heusen; score by Elmer Bernstein and others
Decca DL–71500   1967   Brunswick STA–8685
Star! original motion picture Sound-track, with Daniel Massey, Bruce Forsyth and Beryl Reid; songs by Noel Coward, George and Ira Gershwin and others
Twentieth Century-Fox Records DTCS 5102 *Stereo*   1968
EMI SSL 10233 in Great Britain   1968
Darling Lili: original motion picture Sound-track, with Henry Mancini and his orchestra, Gloria Paul and Le Lysée Français de Los Angeles Children's Choir; new songs composed by Henri Mancini, lyrics by Johnny Mercer
RCA LSPX-1000 *Stereo*   1970   RCA SF–8138
A Little Bit in Love
Harmony H–30021 *Stereo*   1970   or CHM–687
(A reissue from *Broadway's Fair Julie* and *Don't Go into the Lion's Cage Tonight*)
Julie and Carol at Lincoln Centre: original television Sound-track, with Carol Burnett; special material by Mitzi Welch and Ken Welch
Columbia S–31153 *Stereo*   1971
The World of Julie Andrews (In Great Britain: *The Best of Julie Andrews*)
Columbia KG–31970 *Stereo*   1972   CBS–68234
(A reissue from *Broadway's Fair Julie, Don't Go into the Lion's Cage Tonight* and *My Fair Lady* (London cast album)
TV's Fair Julie
Harmony KH–31958 *Stereo*   1972
(A reissue from *Broadway's Fair Julie*)
Secret of Christmas (Great Britain only)
Embassy (CBS) 31237 or 31522   1973

* No longer in catalogue.

215

Julie Andrews
RCA ANL–1–1098 *Stereo*   1975   RCA HY–1002
(A reissue from *Lass with the Delicate Air* and *Julie Andrews Sings*)
An Evening with Julie Andrews (Japan only)
RCA SX–281 (A–7)   1977

Largely Instrumental Sound-tracks from her movies:
The Americanization of Emily: music by Johnny Mandel
Reprise RS–6151 *Stereo*   1964
Torn Curtain: music by John Addison
Decca DL–79155 *Stereo*   1966
Hawaii: music by Elmer Bernstein
United Artists UA–LA283–G *Stereo*   1966
The Pink Panther Strikes Again (Julie sings 'Until You Love Me' in a man's voice)   1976
10: music by Henry Mancini
Warner Brothers BSK 3399 *Stereo*   1979

* No longer in catalogue.

JULIE ANDREWS' MAJOR TELEVISION SHOWS

1. *High Tor*: with Bing Crosby, Nancy Olson; originating network, CBS; produced by Arthur Schwartz; directed by James Neilson; teleplay by Maxwell Anderson (based on his own stage play); music by Arthur Schwartz; lyrics by Maxwell Anderson; 1956.

2. Guest appearance on the Ed Sullivan show, *Toast of the Town*, singing 'I Could Have Danced All Night' and 'Without You' from *My Fair Lady*; CBS; 1956.

3. *Cinderella*: with Edie Adams, Kaye Ballard, Alice Ghostley, Dorothy Stickney, Howard Lindsay, Jon Cypher, Ilka Chase; produced by Richard Rodgers and Oscar Hammerstein II; directed by Ralph Nelson; music by Richard Rodgers, lyrics by Oscar Hammerstein II; sets and costumes by William and Jean Eckart; CBS; 1957.

4. *Crescendo*: ninety-minute special with Rex Harrison as a visiting Englishman entertained by a sampling of most styles of American music; Julie and Stanley Holloway did a medley from *My Fair Lady*; CBS; 1957.

5. Guest appearance on a Jack Benny special, in which she sang 'Ain't We Got Fun' and 'I'm Just Wild About Harry'; CBS; 1960.

6. *Julie and Carol at Carnegie Hall*: with Carol Burnett; produced and directed by Joe Hamilton; special material by Mike Nichols and Ken Welch; choreography by Ernest Flatt; CBS; 1962.

(Emmy Award, and Rose D'Or from Montreaux International Television Festival – the first American programme so honoured. 'We were booed when we won,' Carol Burnett remembered, 'because everyone thought the show was filmed, and of course it was taped. We convinced the audience we had done it in a single performance, and they quieted down.')

7. *The Julie Andrews Show* (colour): with Gene Kelly, the New Christy Minstrels; Alan Handley, producer; Irwin Kostal, musical director; NBC; 1965, repeated 1968. (Two Emmy Awards)'

8. *An Evening with Julie Andrews and Harry Belafonte*: produced and directed by Gower Champion; Michel Legrand, musical director; NBC; 1969.

9. *Julie and Carol at Lincoln Centre*: produced by Joe Hamilton; directed by Dave Powers; special material by Ken and Mitzi Welch; choreography by Ernest Flatt; CBS; 1971.

10. *The Julie Andrews Hour* (series of twenty-four shows): Lew Grade, producer; Bill Davis, director; with Alice Ghostley, Rich Little as regulars, various guest stars; ATV–ABC; September 1972 – March 1973.

(Seven Emmy Awards and Silver Rose Award at Montreux)

11. Julie on *Sesame Street*: with Perry Como and the Muppets; ATV–ABC; 1973.

12. *Julie's Christmas Special*: with Peggy Lee and Peter Ustinov; ATV–ABC; 1973.

13. *Julie and Dick at Covent Garden*: with Dick van Dyke; Blake Edwards, producer and director; ATV–ABC; 1974.

14. *Julie and Jackie – How Sweet It Is*: with Jackie Gleason;

Gary Smith, producer; Dwight Hemion, director; ATV–ABC; 1974.

15. *My Favourite Things*: with Peter Sellers and the Muppets; Blake Edwards, producer and director; ATV–ABC; 1975.

16. *Julie Andrews – One Step into Spring*: with Leslie Uggams and Leo Sayer; CBS; 1978.

17. *The Muppet Show*: ATV – syndicated in USA; 1978.

18. *Julie Andrews' Invitation to the Dance*: with Rudolph Nureyev, Ann Reinking, Green Grass Cloggers; directed by Tony Charmoli; written by Buzz Kohan; CBS; 1980, repeated 1981.

INDEX

221